THE NE

How to win hearts, minds and votes

Claire Ainsley

P

First published in Great Britain in 2018 by

Policy Press
University of Bristol
1-9 Old Park Hill
Bristol
BS2 8BB
UK
t: +44 (0)117 954 5940
pp-info@bristol.ac.uk
www.policypress.co.uk

North America office:
Policy Press
c/o The University of Chicago Press
1427 East 60th Street
Chicago, IL 60637, USA
t: +1 773 702 7700
f: +1 773 702 9756
sales@press.uchicago.edu
www.press.uchicago.edu

© Policy Press 2018

British Library Cataloguing in Publication Data
A catalogue record for this book is available from the British Library.

Library of Congress Cataloging-in-Publication Data
A catalog record for this book has been requested.

ISBN 978-1-4473-4418-6 paperback
ISBN 978-1-4473-4420-9 ePub
ISBN 978-1-4473-4421-6 Mobi
ISBN 978-1-4473-4419-3 ePdf

Cover design by Lyn Davies

"A powerful call to action for policy makers and political leaders to develop coherent and substantive policy programmes that can genuinely engage voters with the democratic system and safeguard it for the future ... systematic and evidence based."
Professor Rosie Campbell, Birkbeck College, University of London

"People on low incomes face so many daily struggles that politics can seem removed and even irrelevant. Claire has hit the nail on the head with this excellent book. Let's hope it encourages a wider debate on our struggling democratic system."
Dann Kenningham, National Coordination, ATD Fourth World

"At its core, this story is about power.... In introducing the new marginalised working class, Claire Ainsley brings impressive clarity and policies to reconnect politicians and ordinary people."
Guy Goodwin, Chief Executive, NatCen Social Research

"This rich and engaging book sets out an ambitious new political and policy agenda, which should be essential reading for anyone hoping to understand and address the working class alienation and disengagement that have disrupted British politics in recent years."
Professor Rob Ford, University of Manchester

For my mum, and everything she stood for.

Contents

v

List of figures

Acknowledgements

I am grateful to the many organisations making their policy and research publicly available, and I have drawn on ideas advocated by the following organisations: Policy Exchange, Joseph Rowntree Foundation, Demos, Social Market Foundation, Resolution Foundation, Institute for Government, Centre for Cities, Shelter, Social Mobility Commission and the Taylor Review on Good Work.

The ideas in the book have been shared with a wide range of people for their feedback, listed below; however, I take full responsibility for the accuracy and opinions expressed. The Office for National Statistics and others like the Institute for Fiscal Studies provide a huge public service by making their data and analysis easily accessible, for which I am grateful. My particular thanks go to NatCen, the National Centre for Social Research, whose British Social Attitudes has formed the basis of the attitudes analysis, and to the Trustees of the Joseph Rowntree Foundation, past and present, for backing the feasibility of the opinion poll and its continuation. I would also like to thank the team at BritainThinks, who have done so much to introduce public insight into political and organisational thinking.

This book compiles the many stories and views of people whose voices run through it. These include low-paid workers and union members during my time at the Transport & General Workers' Union and Unite, community and disabled people's groups, focus groups and participatory workshops, and the Poverty Truth Commissions supported by the Joseph Rowntree Foundation. I would also like to thank my own family and friends for sharing their stories and experiences.

Thanks go to all those who took the time to read all or parts of the manuscript and give me their comments: Rosie Campbell, Mike Savage, James Frayne, Deborah Mattinson, Jon Mellon,

Philip Collins, James Tilley, Oliver Heath, Florence Sutcliffe-Braithwaite, Campbell Robb, Julia Unwin, Jill Rutter, Alan Jones, David Goodhart, Katie Schmuecker, Abigail Scott Paul, Reema Patel, Roger Harding, Patrick South, John Denham, Hayley Rowan, Helen Barnard, Frank Soodeen. My thanks also go to the team at Policy Press, particularly editors Ali Shaw and Dawn Rushen. Thank you to my friends and colleagues at the Joseph Rowntree Foundation and Housing Trust for their support and encouragement; and to my family. My greatest thanks are reserved for Stephen, Joe, and Drew, for their love and understanding. Two people have inspired me more than any others in writing this book: my mum, Sue Ainsley (née Riddle) and Barbara Stewart. Neither of them lived to see this book, but their lives are imprinted throughout.

1

Winning the new working class vote

'In the government's eyes I am invisible.' (Voter, Birmingham)

This story starts in two seaside towns. Clacton-on-Sea, October 2014, scene of the first upset in a run of events in British politics. Conservative MP Douglas Carswell resigned his party and his seat to stand for the UK Independence Party (UKIP), and won re-election with the biggest increase in the share of the vote for any party in any by-election in history. Two years later, Hartlepool, 300 miles up the coast, delivered another political shockwave, but this time, of much greater magnitude. Against all expectations, in June 2016, Britons voted to leave the European Union.

The day after the EU referendum I was sitting in similarly shocked company with colleagues at the Joseph Rowntree Foundation headquarters in York. No one could quite believe it. York had voted solidly to remain in the EU, but it was only one of two places in the whole of North Yorkshire that did not vote to leave. Staff in Hartlepool reported that locals were celebrating. In the subsequent days after the result, the national media descended on places like Hartlepool to discover what had been going on. How could they have misunderstood the mood of the voters so badly? Writer Caitlin Moran calls this the 'Attenboroughisation'[1] of places outside the immediate purview of the London-based media, journalists reporting on these distant 'others' like observers with long-range lenses.

As a result of the referendum the media suddenly became interested in people on lower incomes and those living in parts of the country less well known to them, like Hartlepool and Clacton, because they had turned out to vote against the 'established' view. The referendum result brought into focus the profound disconnection to politics that so many people on low to middle incomes feel. The subsequent characterisation of places 'left behind' by economic globalisation conjured up images of forgotten coastal towns in contrast to the rapid progress of metropolitan cities. Yet this disconnection is not just about places like Hartlepool and Clacton; it is about everywhere. Understanding the political implications of the changing nature of social class in Britain is the start of knowing what can be done about it.

This characterisation of those 'left behind' was compounded by the run-up to the 2017 General Election where the Conservatives made an explicit pitch for what was called the 'working-class' vote, those voters recognised as uncomfortable with Labour's more socially liberal leanings. On election day, the Conservatives had one of their best showings among working-class voters, but had not done enough to win the seats they had targeted. In fact, Labour and the Conservatives picked up an equal split of unclaimed votes of those on lower incomes in 2017 as UKIP's vote collapsed, and the majority of people on low incomes stuck with Labour. In Scotland, sizable parts of this electorate had already dislodged from Labour and voted instead for the Scottish National Party (SNP). It is by no means clear where voters on low to middle incomes will put their votes at future elections, making this a key battleground for all of the major political parties.

What most of the political debate misses is that what is described as 'working class' is actually a much smaller component part of what it means to be working class today. Commentators often talk about the traditional working class, which is a relatively small segment of the population, roughly 14 per cent, but structural changes to the British economy over the past 40 years have created a new working class, which is multi-ethnic, comprised of people living off low to middle incomes, and likely to be occupied in service sector jobs like catering, social care or retail.

Many of them will not define themselves primarily through their work at all. The new working class is more disparate, more atomised, and occupies multiple social identities, which makes collective identity less possible. The trouble for political parties is that none have caught up with modern social class dynamics, let alone understood how demographic and societal changes over the next few years will present them with even more electoral challenges. This book sets out to increase understanding about who the new working class is based on economic, social and cultural factors, and argues that so far, politics has failed to respond to societal change effectively. Based on the views and values of a 'new' working class, I propose a new policy agenda for political parties seeking to attract mass support in Britain.

While it used to be more straightforward to predict the party someone was likely to vote for based on their social class, these days, the association between class and political party has weakened, particularly for working-class voters who used to be much more loyal to Labour. Since 1997, Labour's working-class vote has declined, the Conservatives' has increased, and 'class' has no longer become a reliable signifier of how someone will vote. At the same time, voting patterns among the population according to other characteristics have become more stark. For example, 64 per cent of those aged 18-24 voted Labour in 2017 compared to the Conservatives, who only attracted 20 per cent of this age group's support. The reverse is true of those aged over 60. This pattern was also the case during the EU referendum, when income and class were less of an indicator of how someone voted than their age or whether they had a university degree.

This has led several analysts to conclude that other factors – such as age, education, proximity to a decent job, or in Scotland, national independence – have become the new electoral dividing lines. These analyses are useful and interesting, and add depth and insight into changing demographics and electoral patterns. But these are supplementary rather than a replacement for social class as an explanatory mechanism for British society. None provide a reliable organising principle for a political party seeking a parliamentary majority in the traditional British two-party system. Even in Scotland, nationalism may not provide a sustainable basis for a majority as incumbency factors and interest-based politics play out once again.

> 'I don't understand politics whatsoever.... Never voted, ever. Never, 'cause I don't under.... I don't understand it, I don't understand it.' (Voter, London)

Political parties have been struggling to position themselves in relation to these societal and electoral dynamics. The loss of a collective class identity has prompted some Labour commentators to advocate a shift towards new organising principles away from social class, based on national identity or progressive values. The Conservatives have embarked on a long-term strategy to capture parts of the electorate not associated with their traditional middle to upper class base, and to be seen as a party at ease with representing 'modern' Britain. However, it is not social class per se that has decoupled from party identity, as middle- to upper-class voters are still much more strongly aligned to the Conservative Party.

It is the Labour Party's relationship to working-class voters that has changed the most dramatically, with the most serious consequences realised when the SNP overtook Labour in Scotland at the 2007 Scottish parliamentary elections. In Scotland 'working-class voters' form a majority of the population, and are also decisive in the electoral map of Wales. It is difficult to see how Labour can win a parliamentary majority without a significant shift towards this new working class, and equally, to see how the Conservatives can achieve a majority without taking more substantial numbers of new working-class votes. This is because of the numbers. The new working class isn't some distant grouping. It is comprised of millions and millions of households up and down England, Scotland and Wales who live off an average or below-average income. Not just in Hartlepool, or Clacton-on-Sea, but in every city, every town, every office, shop, high street, pub and place of worship.

Despite significant social and economic progress in the last 40 years, particularly for women, it turns out that we didn't all become middle class. In fact, as wages and living standards continue to be constrained, it is entirely possible that this new

working class will become yet more sizable. While ele
cannot be won on this group alone, as parties mus
coalitions in order to win power, understanding this group
values, attitudes and interests is critical to success in British
politics.

A majority of us today identify as being 'working class', and this
hasn't changed over time. And people's own social class identity
may be different to the given identity chosen by statisticians. This
phenomenon, of being 'working class of the mind', has deep
roots. Some people, who might now even be considered in the
middle or upper groupings, may identify with being working
class due to their background. I have not included these people
in the data, as fundamentally their interests are not what could
truly be classified as 'new' working class; however, it is interesting
to note that in several places someone's 'subjective' working-class
status aligns them to policies that are in the interests of the new
working class. This is an important consideration in building
electoral alliances. It may also reveal the heightened awareness
the British public has for the enduring power of social class in
British society.

A recent poll for the Social Mobility Commission[2] highlighted
that more people think that background and parents determine
where you end up in society than hard work and talent, and this
was much more strongly felt by the under-25s than the over-
65s. In defining this new working class, I have used a number
of sources on demographics, income and class, and built on the
work done by Mike Savage and the team at the Department of
Sociology, London School of Economics and Political Science
(LSE) to identify modern class dynamics through the Great
British Class Survey[3] which returns to an account of 'class' that
incorporates social, cultural and economic factors in determining
someone's class as well as occupation. Throughout the book I
have used the first-hand accounts of people of the 'new' working
class, so their voices come through directly.

Are the concerns and opinions of the new working class so
different to the general public? Generally no, and class and
income doesn't shape or determine every topic. But they do
have particular concerns that do not feature as prominently in
political debate, largely because political debate is preoccupied

with the interests of people on middle to higher incomes. And their attitudes do vary on particular issues. So their priorities and views are somewhat different to those who dominate politics, and politics doesn't look or feel very representative of their perspectives. The topic chapters in this book have been selected using quantitative data of the priorities of people of the new working class, and each chapter outlines the issue from the voters' perspective, before going on to make policy recommendations that would speak to their interests and values.

The values and social identities of voters are incredibly important in understanding the role that policies play in revealing to the electorate who the party or candidate is, and parties could do much better at understanding and appealing to voters' emotions, based on the moral foundations theory put forward by Jonathan Haidt.[4] This, and the role of policies in voter selection, is discussed in Chapter 3. Policies have been selected because the new working class deem the issue a priority, because the policies speak to their concerns, and because there is some efficacy behind them. The book doesn't seek to propose a purely populist agenda, and neither does it select policies because they are what experts think would be good for people on low to middle incomes. The question this book sought to answer is, what would a policy agenda look like based on the concerns and interests of the new working class, which entails both popularity and evidence? It does mean that there has been a cherry picking of attractive policies, but there are also some more profound reforms included, and I have confessed in the concluding chapter the areas I ducked because public opinion was so far off-side. Clearly any policy would need further testing with voters and more extensive expert scrutiny before including in a programme, but for the purposes of this book, I hope they provide the reader with food for thought about what matters to people.

'Be honest – tell the people what you are going to do, and just do it.' (Voter, North Shields)

A politics to win the hearts, minds and votes of the new working class demands a series of democratic reforms designed to bring about political equality. In Chapter 7, ideas are put forward to strengthen the democratic representation of the new working class, and a new model for public attitudes-led policy-making is proposed. There is a sophisticated industry around polling and voter insight, but this is primarily used to the benefit of political parties and private clients. There is a strong case that it should be used for public benefit and policy-making, as part of a series of measures to open up the process of determining priorities and actions. Politicians should not just introduce policies because public support indicates that they would be popular, nor avoid policies just because there is no public support. But starting with what the public think – and not just the new working class – does suggest what the priorities should be, what the views of the public are, what the likely vote winners are, and demonstrates where ground needs to be laid for important but less popular policies.

Policy is more likely to stick for the long term if there is the public will to support it, and policy-making would be much stronger if it embedded the lived experience of people who use and administer public services right the way through the process. It is hard to look at the politics and policy-making of today and not conclude that ordinary people, rather than professional lobbyists or politicians, have been excluded from the process. Can you imagine how different it would be if Universal Credit, the new welfare system, had been conceived of and designed with the people who need and administer it? There are some interesting attempts to calibrate services alongside people, but unless there is real political equality for people on low to middle incomes, these attempts will be transactional rather than about sharing power.

In the concluding chapter, the new policy agenda based on the values of the new working class is drawn together. Based on the public's own values of family, fairness, hard work and decency, policies are set out that are grounded in the priorities, values and attitudes of the new working class. They position the role of the state as being the guarantor of basic services, and the individual takes a more defined role in contributing to life costs. They require a more active business and employer interest in societal good, matching employer need for skills and favourable

7

conditions with investing in Britain's future through schools, colleges and good work. They demand a much longer-term perspective from government, employers and citizens to meet the demographic changes of our future population, to ensure that we are a prosperous nation as well as one whose prosperity is more evenly shared.

There is also quite a lot the book recommends politicians of all political parties should stop doing. All political parties are guilty of talking to themselves too much, and assuming that their ideological frame of reference relates to voters more than it actually does. Taking an ideological view of the state – either to shrink it or expand it – does not enable good policy. And hobby horses like fox hunting and the legalisation of cannabis are just baffling to most voters.

During the writing of this book I have grappled with definitions of 'class' and wrestled with reams of data. But when I think about who the new working class is, I do not see dots on a graph. I do not think about whether someone's income or social capital pushes them over an imaginary line that makes them new working class or not. I see the face of my friend Barbara, a black disabled woman who contributed more to her community in East London than anyone who was paid to, but who could not realise her capability in case she lost her right to an income. I hear the voices of the young women in Glasgow I listened to while they told a group that they bought trainers they could not afford to impress people they did not like for fear of being shamed for their lack of money. I think of the trade union members I met in South Wales who were trying to keep a community together the morning after I had witnessed stories of the exploitation of Eastern European agency workers. I remember the cleaners I worked with to secure better terms and conditions from agencies serving some of the biggest corporations in the world. I picture someone I love, but she's complaining about the number of immigrants using the health service, when migrant workers helped care for her. What do any of these people have in common with one another, let alone people in Clacton or in Hartlepool? They do not have a collective identity; some are downright hostile to one another. But the one thing they share is that they have been poorly served by democracy, and none of the political parties are speaking for them now. In the minds of those close to power, their voices are marginal. But their numbers are considerable and they have an equal right to be heard. Sometimes their interests will differ, but more often than not I found that the same policies speak to the concerns and interests of the new working class. Perhaps most persuasively, I do not think there is a route to power without them.

The changes in society we are currently undergoing are profound, and our politics needs to catch up. In the next few years we will become increasingly diverse as a society. Divisions between age are likely to become even more politically important, as people's understanding of the state's role and their own wealth accumulation alters between generations. Digital technology is rapidly changing the way we live, work and shop, and established institutions are finding themselves outpaced by competitors who are more aligned to the public's needs. We can already see that people's expectations of having a say in their lives are increasing, but the gap between those who have political power and representation may only widen if it is not addressed more directly. The rise and fall of UKIP is far less instructive than the rise and rise of the SNP, which outpaced and outmanoeuvred the political institution that was the Scottish Labour Party. There are warning signs from Europe and North America, too, of the failure of democracies to adapt politically to societal and economic change, from the election of Donald Trump as US President to the close call of Marine Le Pen being presidential runner-up in France.

This is not a battle cry from the 'left behind', whoever that is, but the story of what it means to be part of the working class in Britain today, in its multiple forms, why it matters politically, and how parties should respond. If any political party wants to win a parliamentary majority, they need to understand and speak to the concerns and interests of the new working class. This book will set out why political parties should, and how they can do it.

2

Who are the new working class?

'I see myself as a working hard person, trying to provide for a family.' (Voter, Edinburgh)

In today's society, 'class' can seem an outmoded concept, with distinctions between the social classes becoming more blurred over time. Collective identities appear to have given way to more individualised forms of expression. Most of us want to be seen for who we feel we are, not defined by the background or circumstances we were born into. But even if we accept social class exists in Britain today, which most people recognise, does it actually matter?

This book argues that class does matter, but it has changed. The British economy and society has been fundamentally re-made during the course of the latter part of the 20th century, and while the traditional working class has declined in form and number, a new working class is emerging. In politics, class really matters, and the political articulation of social class through the parties has been one of the defining features of British politics. Political parties that fail to transform with economic and social change risk long-term decline. Yet the tectonic plates in society have shifted again in the last 40 years, and none of the major parties have been adept enough at understanding that shift and responding politically. This book sets out to tell the story of the emergence of the new working class, charting its composition and interests, and offering a political strategy rooted in its values and attitudes. More than anything, this book is an appeal to political parties to listen to the concerns of these voters and to act on them.

'Hard working families' and the 'just about managing'

Social class is central to understanding politics, but politicians have generally shied away from using the overt language of 'class', preferring opaque groupings like 'hard working families'. Even when political leaders mentioned class in the past, it tended to be in terms that leaders defined themselves against. Winston Churchill in opposition used class to denounce the government: 'The driving force of Socialism is class hatred and envy'.[1] Forty-five years later, Tony Blair claimed that the 'class system, unequal and antiquated' had been part of a past that had defined the nation, and declared that 'The class war is over.'[2] Even John Major, a politician who probably understood the British class system more than most, famously called for a 'classless society'.[3] Ed Miliband made no reference to class in any of his speeches.[4]

Political rhetoric has featured new groupings and categorisations, designed to demonstrate the party's affiliation to the voters they wish to attract. 'Hardworking families' entered political discourse in the UK in late 1990s,[5] and usage of the term peaked during the 2005 General Election campaign. Theresa May set out her appeal to a new category – the 'just about managing'[6] – in her first speech as Prime Minister in 2016. This then gave way to a hybrid 'ordinary working families', which Cabinet Minister Justine Greening defined as those who are ineligible for the pupil premium,[7] but living below a median income.[8] In the run-up to the 2017 General Election, May rediscovered the language of class in a direct appeal to disenfranchised traditional working-class voters, recognising a gap in the market. Nick Clegg tried the phrase 'alarm-clock Britain', which did not catch on, while Ed Miliband had more success with the phrase the 'squeezed middle', capturing a phenomenon that was repeated in public discourse.

The function of these phrases is primarily rhetorical devices rather than a shift in political orientation to social class, although 'just about managing' was at least underpinned by a targeted voter strategy.[9] Taken together, the phrases give the impression of political leaders searching for a sound bite to make them come across as in touch with everyday concerns, rather than reflecting a deep understanding of the changing nature of modern Britain.

Political decline of the working class

In politics, as in life generally, not all classes are equal. While politicians tend not to use the language of class, this is not to say that they do not still use the politics of class. Voters in the lowest income group are much more likely to say no party represents them (24 per cent compared to just 6 per cent in the highest income group[10]). Those in the highest income group are much more likely to say they identify with the Conservatives (46 per cent) than those on the lowest incomes saying they identify with Labour (30 per cent).[11] Interests have not detached from political allegiance per se; it is party identification with Labour by class and income that has broken down most significantly, and voters in the lower to middle income ranges who are much more likely not to feel represented by any party.

In the 1980s, Labour, under Neil Kinnock, identified that their 'natural' support base had declined in real terms.[12] In 1982, even before he became an MP, future Prime Minister

Figure 1: Identifying with a political party

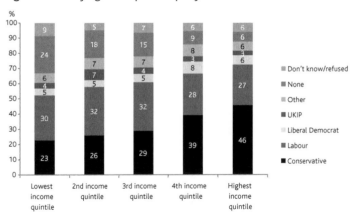

Source: Taylor et al (2017)

Tony Blair wrote that Anthony Crosland had been right in 1956 when he identified 'major alterations in British society; in particular, the rise in living standards of sections of the working class and the emergence of a new white collar class.'[13] It was argued that in the 1950s Labour had been too slow to respond to the changing class dynamics of a more affluent society.[14] As leader, Blair often said that the reason that Labour lost between 1979 and 1992 was that 'society had changed and we did not change sufficiently with it.'[15] Labour's political strategy in the 1990s was to respond to changing social structures by courting the middle class, particularly former working-class voters who had become affluent homeowners.[16] For Blair, the route to parliamentary victory was to 'own the future' and go with the grain of social change: 'Create more people with more income and more education, they are going to want to make more choices; hence the importance of tax as an issue for the aspiring working class as well as the middle class.'[17] By appealing to voters' aspirations, shoring up Labour's economic credentials as a party of government, and exploiting the Conservatives' weaknesses after 18 years in power, Blair's New Labour won 43.2 per cent of the vote, and consigned the Conservatives to the longest period of opposition in their history.

Figure 2: How the working class voted, 1964-2015

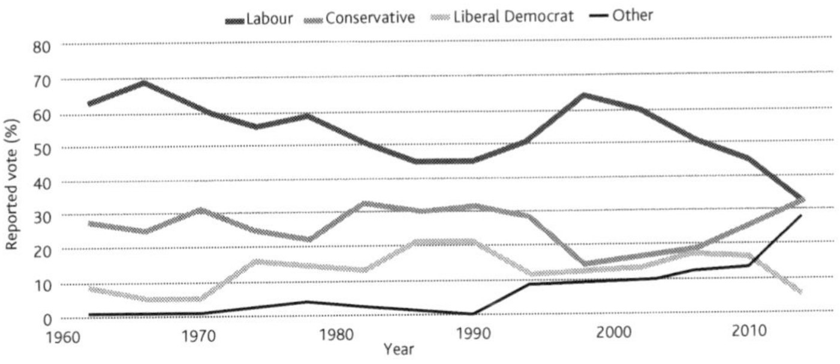

Source: Goodwin and Heath (2017)

But by Labour's third successive victory in 2005, working-class support for Labour had waned, and non-voting rates of working-class voters increased.[18] Over time the class divide in rates of voting became greater than the class divide in the choice between the two main UK parties.[19] By 2010, it is argued (not least by Blair himself) that Labour had lost touch with the public more generally and with their anxieties.[20] What New Labour had done so powerfully at its inception – to bring together insight, policy, people and communication – seemed out of reach after 13 years in power. But the public was changing, and this time it was not becoming more affluent and more middle class; a new working class was emerging. Meanwhile, thinkers on the centre-right began coming up with ideas for how the Conservatives could broaden their appeal from their traditional base, such as Renewal's publication, *Access all areas*.[21] While these ideas did not gain sufficient traction under the David Cameron-led Conservative Party, Theresa May's pitch to the 'just about managing' reaped some benefit in 2017 when the Conservatives began to show a slight increase in support in traditional working-class areas. The argument that once was so powerfully put by Blair that Labour had not sufficiently changed with society is once again made here, but this time it is the new working class that Labour has failed to respond fast enough to.

The political marginalisation of the British working class has been compounded by the dominance in public life in recent times of what the writer David Goodhart calls the 'anywheres': social and economic liberals, university-educated, with professional jobs, in the upper quartile of the income and class spectrum, comfortable with immigration, European integration and the spread of human rights legislation. And politics has orientated to meet their interests: 'where the interests of anywheres are at stake – in everything from reform of higher education to gay marriage – things happen. Where they are not, the wheels grind more slowly, if at all.'[22] The interests of the 'somewheres' – lower to middle incomes, not university-educated, older, living in small towns and suburbia, who value security and nostalgia, and who are numerically larger but with a weaker political voice – are overshadowed by the politically and economically entitled. Even if the categorisations are pretty general,[23] the point it underlines is that the interests of a narrow but entitled minority have come to dominate everyone else's, leading to a dislocation between the mass of society and its political representation by the major parties.

The answer to understanding this decoupling of political identity from class-based interests lies partly in understanding the softness of the working-class vote that has not been solidly Labour-loyal – there have always been working-class Conservatives. The answer also lies in understanding that Labour in government did not manage to successfully sustain the alliance Neil Kinnock had hoped to build between traditional working-class voters and the growing middle class.[24] Whether through policy or politics, Labour's failure to face both ways caused a fracture that only an understanding of how class was being fundamentally re-made during this period can hope to heal. By 2015, Labour had lost its lead among working-class voters, which were roughly split between the two main parties; UKIP and the SNP took nearly 30 per cent of the working-class vote between them.[25] New Labour was right to suppose that Labour could not build a parliamentary majority based on the traditional working-class vote alone, but they were wrong to assume those voters would have nowhere else to go.

'A big dream of mine would be to own my own house. I think it was wonderful what Margaret Thatcher did for people back in the 1980s, letting them buy their own home. All right, they're all sold up now, but that doesn't mean they couldn't build some more, does it? I don't know how I'm going to pay for my kids to go to university. That's something I'd like for them to do. I think they want to learn and get ahead but I just don't know how I could do it, financially.'
(Voter, Essex)

Re-making British society

Understanding the scale and experience of social and economic change in Britain in the past four decades is crucial to understanding the political dislocation of class. As a nation, we are more populated, more diverse, more socially liberal, more urban, more likely to be employed, more educated, consume more, and are living longer. Many of the changes that have taken place have increased opportunity and prosperity, but the benefits have been felt very unevenly. Income disparity is far higher today, and nearly one-third of the population lives below what is considered a Minimum Income Standard to participate in society.[26] Some have experienced upward social mobility, but overall social mobility is perceived to be declining,[27] with millions of workers required to fill the lower-skilled jobs that have replaced the mid-level jobs of the past. The experience of profound change, continually portrayed by the dominant political narratives as progress, has left 68 per cent of working-class people agreeing with the statement, 'Britain has changed for the worse over the past 20-30 years.'[28]

The experience of work, brought about by changes to the UK's macro-economy, is, of course, at the very centre of this change. The deindustrialisation that began in the 1980s and continues to this day has completely altered the prospects and politics of the UK's working class. The number of working-age adults in employment is at a record high, but the nature of the work they do has changed in response to global competition and technology, reducing the relative size and labour-intensiveness of the UK's manufacturing base. Today's workers are much more likely to be employed in the UK's service industries, which account for 79 per cent of GDP.[29]

While the effect of comparatively lower wages has been mitigated by the introduction of the National Minimum Wage in 1998, the statutory minimum (now called the 'National Living Wage') is not enough to guarantee a decent standard of living due to rising costs and eroding in-work state support.[30]

Meanwhile, the number of mid-level jobs has shrunk, and the opportunities to progress are curtailed. The minimum has not turned out to be the 'starter' rate it was intended to be, and millions of workers are stuck in low pay with little prospect of escaping. A study of low-paid workers found that only one in six of those surveyed managed to escape low pay over the course of a decade.[31] The distribution of wealth and assets is not just uneven between social classes, but between genders, ethnicities, abilities and generations, with today's working-age and younger people much less likely to own their own assets than previous generations. Those aged 65–74 now hold more wealth than the entire population aged under 45, a group more than twice their size.[32] The changing pattern of asset accumulation has profound and far-reaching political consequences, as it shapes the relationships individuals have to the economy, not just based on how they are employed, but when they happened to be born.

'My contract is four hours a week but I do 30 hours a week ... so I don't get a pension, and when I went on maternity leave I couldn't take my full leave because of my four-hour contract.' (Voter, Slough)

Patterns of work as well as the nature and location of employment have changed dramatically. In general people are more likely to change jobs, careers and employers more frequently than they used to, which has a practical, material impact as well as one of affiliation and belonging. Part-time, shift and contract working is much more prevalent. While increased flexibility – of hours, location and shared parental care – has undoubtedly been to the benefit of many workers, families and employers, the effects have been variable. Increased self-employment has allowed many workers to cut out the profit made by a manager or shop owner, but for others, typically on lower incomes, self-employment has been a means for more unscrupulous employers to evade statutory responsibilities. Increased zero hours' contracts have enabled some workers to balance their work and home commitments, but for others, they have led to financial insecurity. A small but increasing number of workers has been left without basic employment provisions such as paid sick pay and occupational maternity pay. The decline in union density as newer industries replace more heavily unionised sectors has had a negative impact on job security as well as on terms and conditions, and worker self-organisation has been restricted by anti-union legislation.

One of the most significant changes in the post-war period is the role of women in the British economy and society, with more women in paid work than ever before. Family formations have diversified from the traditional set-up of a sole male breadwinner, and the expectation these days, certainly from the way state

Income Support is structured, is that households will have dual earners. Greater equality has created better opportunities for women in life and work, but the jobs typically done by women are usually less well paid, partly due to society's value judgements, and because family and caring responsibilities still fall unduly on women, making promotion or full-time work sometimes not worth the additional burden.[33] More women in work has occurred as the relative employment of men has declined, and the average age of a worker has risen due to people living longer. As technological developments bring about changes in the way we live and work, the effects of automation are likely to be felt keenly by those employed in routine work, who are more likely to be women, and may lack the job mobility to diversify due to lower labour market skills.

'It's about 20p an hour more to be a senior care assistant, but you could get sued or go to prison because you're giving out medication, which you don't do at my level.' (Voter, Grimsby)

Black, Asian and minority ethnic workers face persistent disadvantages in employment. Some minority ethnic groups are segregated into certain low-skilled occupation types, compared to a relatively even distribution of White British workers, with significant differences between and within minority ethnic groups. Unemployment rates are particularly high for men and women in the ethnic group White Gypsy/Irish Traveller, men in the Other Black and Mixed White-Caribbean groups, and Bangladeshi, Arab and Pakistani women.[34] The typical Bangladeshi household income is 35 per cent (£8,900 a year) lower than the White British median, for example, and Bangladeshi women have just a 31 per cent rate of employment compared to 72 per cent of White British women.[35] Poverty is up to twice as likely among some minority ethnic groups as it is for White people.[36]

The backdrop to this disadvantage in the labour market is persistent discrimination faced by black, Asian and minority ethnic people, which restricts racial equality in work, education and wider society. It is also part of the reason that first- and second-generation migrants may experience downward mobility on entry to the UK, compared to their nation of origin.[37] The dynamics of unevenly distributed chances in the labour market due to gender, disability and race are reflective of wider societal inequalities that concentrate power and opportunity.

The way we work has changed, our households have changed, and so, too, have the places we live in. Cities have been the centres of economic growth, particularly London, with its world-leading financial services sector. Yet while they have accumulated income and wealth, they are physically segregated by class and income, a pattern replicated outside of London: in Greater Manchester, for example, 82 per cent of the city's elite live in one-quarter of the city's postcodes.[38] Social integration between groups on the basis of ethnic origin, faith, income and by social class is uneven.

The rising demand for public services brought about by an ageing population and increased migration has disproportionately fallen to less prosperous areas. Most migrants fill labour shortages (approximately one-third of doctors are non-British born, for example), but overall, migrants have a slightly higher tendency to be unemployed.[39] The social and political impact of increased immigration into the UK in recent years has been even more profound than the economic impact. It was one of the factors behind the vote to leave the EU, with a proportion of voters uneasy with the pace of increased migration flows.

Britain is a changing nation, and social attitudes have changed with it over a relatively short period of time. Generally, social attitudes have become more liberal and socially accepting of difference. Significant freedoms for women, minority ethnic groups, people with disabilities, and lesbian, gay, bisexual and transgender people have been brought about, sometimes accompanied by legislative change. While discrimination is still present and told through this story, most people support the progress in social equality that has been achieved, and that is broadly consistent across social classes.[40] Having said that, there are strong undercurrents and social fractures revealed by the vote to leave the EU that have caused many to question the extent to which Britain is a nation at ease with itself.

Understanding the 'new' working class

As the nature of work and modern life has changed so dramatically, then so, too, must our understanding of social class. None of the changes that have taken place mean that class is less relevant, but as a relative concept, it needs to be remade in response. The working class as a relatively clear group of people in society, with a common economic experience and cultural identity, has been fractured by the changes of the past few decades. Instead, a new working class is emerging, as sizable as its historical predecessor, and as in need of political and workplace representation, but it is more disparate, more atomised, and occupies multiple social identities that make collective identity less possible. Its dominance in the shape and structure of society and the economy is as powerful as it has ever been, but it is different to what has gone before, and requires a fresh understanding of modern social class dynamics to appreciate its political power. This book does not advocate that political parties solely appeal to the new working class, but that a parliamentary majority is unlikely unless this population is understood, both demographically and attitudinally.

Social class is not a fixed concept but a construct with a purpose dependent on context. Categorising people is not a neutral exercise, but one laden with a desire to define and differentiate one group compared to another. The reason can depend on the politics and intent of the author or speaker. For Karl Marx, class is primarily defined by the relationship to the means of production,[41] and defining class in this way was intended to serve the purpose of mobilising political action. E.P. Thompson argued in the classic *The making of the English working class*[42] that class is not an objective category but actively made by its participants, 'something which in fact happens (and can be shown to have happened) in human relationships', rather than a structure or a category. For Pierre Bourdieu, social order is perpetuated by acquired or inherited class-based attributes that form social and cultural capital, reinforcing existing structures through the way people behave as well as through language.[43] Formal classifications may seem more neutral than these accounts, but they, too, can be politically or culturally loaded, and ought always to be assessed themselves for the context and motive of the proponent. For the purposes of this book, social class is used as a means to identify and activate political interest in a large grouping, which has been marginalised due to the significant political, social and economic change that has taken place since 1980.

The first efforts to formally classify British society were in the early 19th century, as middle-class professionals became preoccupied with the character of, and their placement in relation to, the newer, well-paid, skilled artisans and other white-collar workers.[44] The Registrar General's Office devised the first classifications by household in 1911, a move that was also driven by the desire to identify poor households, as poverty came to be understood as predominantly the product of social conditions rather than individual failure, following the studies of Charles Booth in London and Seebohm Rowntree in York.[45] Rather than being based on occupation alone, these early classifications grouped types of job according to 'culture', because of the association between hygiene and lower mortality of the poorest. In *Social class in the 21st century*, Mike Savage says that social ranking was therefore a means to make cultural judgements: 'The origins of class classification … cannot be removed from this elitist concern to demarcate and map the boundary of respectability, seen predominantly to differentiate middle (non-manual) and working (manual) classes … the underlying concern was with the cultural and moral aspects of class.'[46] John Goldthorpe's sociological analysis of class in the 1970s led to a new occupational class scheme, which is the basis of the one used by official statisticians today.[47] The scheme allowed for a more rigorous explanation of the divisions between different occupational types, and removed moral or cultural judgements.

More recently, Savage's sociological analysis of the Great British Class Survey (GBCS) has provided a fresh take on the composition of social class in Britain in the 21st century. Rather than use 'occupation' as the sole or dominant contributory factor to a person's class, Savage applies Bourdieu's argument that social class arises from three kinds of capital: economic (wealth and income); cultural (tastes, interests and activities); and social (social networks, friendships and associations). Savage argues that social class in the 21st century is being fundamentally re-made, with a class order that is more hierarchical in differentiating the top (the 'elite') from the bottom (the 'precariat', a phrase first coined by Guy Standing[48]). In between these two extremes lie five other social classes – the established middle class; technical middle class; new affluent workers; traditional working class; and emerging service workers – and the boundaries between them are more blurred.

The purpose of this new analysis is to provide an illustration of social class today that goes beyond occupation, and one that represents the multiple facets involved in understanding class, rather than a replacement for the occupation-based scheme. Building on the notion that background plays a role in class identity, Savage demonstrates how the accumulation of the different kinds of capital contribute to class position, therefore class identity becomes dynamic rather than a static 'point in time'. Historic advantages and disadvantages build up over time. These are social and cultural as much as they are economic, as well-educated people are able to advance their causes with institutions and navigate markets to get the best service. In her book about the personal experience of changing social classes, Lynsey Hanley describes the 'silent symbols' within culture, more powerful than money, as 'keys that can't be bought.'[49] Those without educational resources may feel under-qualified, or even ashamed, unable to make themselves clearly and effectively heard. Savage cites Bourdieu's study of cultural capital to underline how the privileged and the powerful use their connections to help each other and protect their interests, using their 'weak ties' to convey benefits.[50]

According to public perception research, the public perceive occupation and financial status to be the key determinants of someone's social class, but acknowledge factors such as whether someone went to a state or private school, and the social class of their parents, in contributing to someone's class position.[51] Reflecting the views of the public, this book primarily uses material factors of occupation and financial status in defining the new working class, but finds that traditional occupation-based schemes do not fully represent what it means to be working class today.

Numerically, the size of the working class has shrunk, according to the Office for National Statistics (ONS) regarding occupation-based class schemes (accounting for around a quarter of the population).[52] However, this does not reflect the reality of the modern British economy and society in that a large section of the population lives off low to mid incomes, who may not share a unified identity or social and cultural experience, but who have a similarity of economic and financial experience compared to those who are better off. For them, work tends to be non-graduate and less well paid, and more difficult to progress in. While some on lower individual incomes will be living in a household with someone on a higher income, in general, they are more likely to find they can only 'just manage' financially. Overwhelmingly, they will be less likely to have a university degree than those on higher incomes. A proportion will either not be working due to health or caring responsibilities, or will be moving in and out of work. Many would not define themselves primarily through work at all. Overall people on lower to middle incomes are more likely than those on higher incomes to be female, younger, have a disability, and be from a minority ethnic group, with significant variation between ethnicities in income and experience. They are more likely to rely on public services such as health, schools, social security, the police and social services; to be renting rather than homeowners; and to be less insulated from market forces such as rising costs and less secure work.

The main reason social class distinctions have become so blurred is because work has changed so dramatically since there was a more cemented view of class closely associated with occupation. The new working class undertakes hundreds of different types of jobs in today's economy, employed as cleaners, shop workers, bar tenders, cooks, carers, teaching assistants, secretaries, delivery workers, and so on. Many of the jobs that have emerged and taken the place of traditional routine jobs could hardly be called middle class now. These workers may have formal full-time contracts, but are more likely than professional workers to work part time with different hours and shifts, sometimes by choice, sometimes not. More recently, they are more likely than they were to be self-employed without a formal employer. Or the

Figure 3: Profile of income groups by age, gender and education

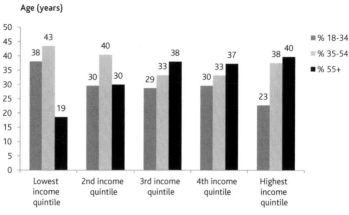

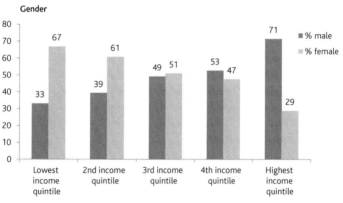

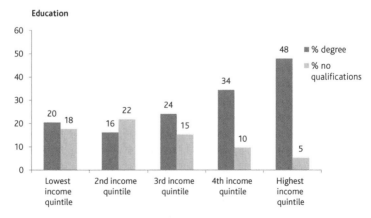

Source: Taylor et al (2017)

place they work in every day may be different to the firm that employs them, because they are contract workers. There is also a reasonable proportion who combine work with caring and other responsibilities, or who don't work at all.

Too many people in the new working class are trapped by receiving an education that did not equip them well enough in the first place, into jobs that do not pay enough to make ends meet, and are stuck there due to lack of opportunity and skills to move on. As the opening chapter states, the new working class is multi-ethnic, of all abilities, and more likely to be female than male. If there ever was a 'typical' working-class person previously, there certainly isn't now.

We can build up a richer picture of the new working class loosely based on the definitions outlined in the GBCS. Using this scheme, the new working class is made up of the traditional working class (representing approximately 14 per cent of the population), emerging service workers (19 per cent) and the 'precariat' (15 per cent). It excludes the elite (6 per cent) and the established middle class (25 per cent). It is possible that some members of the technical middle class (6 per cent) and new affluent workers (15 per cent) might identify as working class depending on their background and societal association, but they are not core to the definition of the new working class. Taken together, these groups equal roughly 48 per cent of the population.

The exact proportions and attributes are less important than the descriptive power of using social and cultural characteristics to supplement income and wealth. The traditional working class has an average age of 66, and is less likely to be from a minority ethnic origin than emerging service workers or new affluent workers. The average household income is well below the median, at £13,000 per year. However, their accumulated wealth (savings plus house value) is more than that of new affluent workers, as well as the classes below (emerging service workers and the 'precariat'). They are likely to enjoy a reasonable level of 'highbrow' cultural capital, captured in reported participation in cultural forms such as visiting museums or art galleries. They are likely to have high social contact with other people, but are more limited in the number of people they know outside of their own class compared to other groups. Emerging service workers are younger (average age 32), more likely to be educated, 21 per cent from a minority ethnic group (compared to 9 per cent of the traditional working class), with the highest emerging cultural capital of any group and considerable social networks, but not much economic capital. They are much more likely than other groups to use social media, enjoy contemporary culture and take part in sport and fitness.

At the bottom is the 'precariat', which has by far the lowest household income, little, if any, savings, is more likely to rent property, with a narrower range of social ties, few associates in higher-status occupations, and more limited highbrow cultural capital, but they are culturally engaged with social networks in their community. Guy Standing described this group as people who are living and working precariously, usually in a series of short-term jobs, but not always the ones selected for low-paid service work, to serve coffee, clean or look after children, when there are able workers from overseas. Rather than being typically workless, these people are more likely to be claiming unemployment benefits in between poorly paid, insecure work. They are the subjects of a negative public discourse, at times vilified and looked down on by the rest of society.

Figure 4: New working class groupings

	Traditional working class	Emerging service workers	Precariat
% of population	14	19	15
Annual household income	£13k	£21k	£8k
Household savings	£10k	£1k	£1k
House value	£127k	£18k	£27k
Average age	66	32	50
% minority ethnic	9	21	13
% graduates	11	18	4

Source: Savage (2015)

Despite several decades of a shrinking and politically marginalised traditional working class, a majority of the British public still identify as working class. Initially most people say they do not belong to a class, although prompted or unprompted more say they are working class than middle class (when asked to choose, 60 per cent say working class compared to 40 per cent saying middle class).[53] The proportion who consider themselves working class has not changed since 1983.[54] While this does not suggest that there is an active working-class identity, it does suggest that we did not all become middle class; therefore to assume the electorate all aspire to be middle class is a misreading of how people feel.

A proportion of those who self-identify as working class would be middle class or even elite by today's standards, but may associate themselves with being working class because of their family background or origins. Geoffrey Evans and Jon Mellon, writing for NatCen, call this 'the working class of the mind.'[55] At the same time, people who might objectively be considered working class may self-identify as middle class or shun class labels altogether.[56] Understanding concerns about identity is absolutely crucial to British politics, but social class does not offer a straightforward proposition to politicians to deploy. For the purposes of this book, a definition of the new working class has been chosen that is based more on material factors than self-identity. One of the interesting factors to note is that policies that appeal to new working-class voters tend to have higher support among those who consider themselves to be working class (subjective class status) than those who do not, suggesting that there may sometimes be opportunities to align ideology and interests for electoral gain.

'I would say working middle.... I see myself as a working hard person, trying to provide for a family, because I come from a working background, I don't see myself upper because I don't think I class myself as being a snob, a label or anything associated with that type of person, associating with free loading money. I would say that I'm – definitely, I'm working class, down to earth if I'm honest.' (Voter, Edinburgh)

The new working class is not one cohesive, monolithic whole, but comprised of the constituent parts of what it means to be working class today. It is not unified by collective identity or culture, but does share some similarities of economic and financial experience. It is politically unequal, yet constitutes around half of the population. For political parties seeking a parliamentary majority, it is essential to their success that they understand what this new working class is, its experiences, attitudes and values, and how it should appeal to them. While there will be tensions and trade-offs at times between the interests and outlook of some of these groups, more often than not the broad approaches that will work for and appeal to these groups share common components. Those policies form the substantive part of this book, based on what voters say are their political and social priorities.

The first rule of the new working class

British people are acutely aware of class. They may prefer not to define themselves by it, but they know it exists, that it plays a central role in society, and this has not changed over time. When asked whether people think of themselves as belonging to any particular class, around half will initially say no.[57] This is roughly the same proportion as in the 1960s,[58] when class demarcations were seen as very strong. Moreover, 73 per cent say that it is 'very' or 'fairly' difficult to move between classes, a figure that has actually risen from 65 per cent a decade ago, and 77 per cent say the differences between the classes are 'very' or 'fairly' wide.[59] A majority of people perceive that there are class divisions and boundaries in British society, and people who identify as working class are more likely to be aware of the divisions and boundaries. Most people – whether middle or working class – think it has become more difficult to move between classes. British society is still shaped by class, and people understand that, because they experience the economic, social and cultural implications. While politicians have gone cool on identifying with and representing working-class voters, there has long been an element of popular culture that ridicules the idea of being 'posh'. Class is alive and well, and present in our everyday experiences.

The perception of the rigidity of social class is borne out by reality. Only 4 per cent of doctors, 6 per cent of barristers and 11 per cent of journalists are from working-class origins.[60] The GBCS shows that the elite come from the most advantaged backgrounds, starting out with high economic, cultural and social capital that becomes mutually reinforcing with other members of the elite. The opposite is true for those at the bottom of the social classes: 65 per cent of the precariat class remain where they started.[61] Just 5 per cent of children from the worst-off backgrounds gain 5 A grades at GCSE, having been 27 times more likely to go to an inadequate school than the least disadvantaged.[62] From those who do achieve the same GCSE results, one-third more of the worst-off children drop out of post-16 education than their better-off classmates.[63] While there is some movement between those who came from manual worker backgrounds into the new affluent workers, the biggest social determinant of class is where you started out.[64]

Britain's social mobility problem is not getting better despite decades of policy designed to improve it.[65] Researchers Jo Blanden and Stephen Machin at the Centre for Economic Performance at LSE found that income mobility had, in fact, declined for generations born in 1970 compared with those born in 1958, largely due to the children of better-off families having disproportionately benefited from the expansion of higher education.[66]

Herein is an irony that is vital for political strategists to grasp: to misappropriate the words of Tyler Durden in Fight Club, *the first rule of the new working class is you do not talk about the new working class*. Despite the evident reality that social background is the key determinant in predicting someone's prospects, suggesting this denies all sense of individual agency.[67] Who wants to be defined by their background, especially if their background has declining prospects? And the term 'working class' itself can be hard to connect with if you do not primarily see yourself through your occupation, or if you do not have one. If you are a part-time female worker, or have a disability and are reliant on state support, or simply do not associate with the term for its perceived narrowness of ethnicity or place, it can be alienating rather than a positive identity to associate with.

While this book argues that class is still the most useful lens through which to view political interests, it is also important to recognise that other aspects of identity, such as age, gender, race and education, matter to who we are, how we see ourselves and what our attitudes are. In fact, while class and income had an association with how people voted in the referendum on leaving the EU, education had the strongest correlation in determining whether people voted to leave or not.[68] Because of the deep cleavages in how different sections of society voted, the EU referendum has shone a spotlight on some of the divisions and tensions in the UK.

Jeremy Cliffe declared in 2014 that 'the great divide is not north versus south or cities versus towns or left versus right, or even working-class versus middle class. It is between those communities that have found a way to thrive in the economic circumstances conscribing England today ... and those that have not been able or (debatably) willing to do so.'[69] This proposition has been developed further by Will Jennings and Gerry Stoker as describing 'Two Englands' of cosmopolitan, urban areas, and shrinking, provincial settings.[70] However, academics at Nuffield College have identified that attitudes between social classes were fairly divided on important questions even 40 years ago, such as on immigration, Europe and having no say in politics.[71] There are deep divisions in British society, but they are not that new. Given the fragmented character of the new working class, the term itself cannot be viewed as a rallying call, because there is not a strong enough collective affiliation to it to make it useful in political communications.

It is precisely because social class matters so much that it can conspire against rather than liberate, that using the term politically can be self-defeating. The purpose of identifying this new working class is to highlight its overlooked experience, its values, attitudes and policy preferences, to inform political strategy aimed at winning a parliamentary majority. The question of how to communicate lies in activating its moral frames, shared values, attitudes and interests, to which we now turn.

3

Do policies matter?

'We are only consulted during election time when the politicians want to win voters, otherwise it's the same people involved in the decision-making processes and politicians only move in their own circles.' (Voter, Oldham)

Much of this book is devoted to policies, defined as the plan of action set out by political parties in government or opposition, so the reader can correctly assume that the starting premise of the book is that *policies do matter*. The question is posed because conventional democratic theory and practice can misstate the role of policies in voter behaviour. There is no straightforward correlation between social and economic interests and how people vote: in fact, political parties are often at odds with the policy preferences of the people who vote for them.[1] This chapter sets out the role and relative significance of policies in voter choice, and in the context of this new working class, argues that understanding people's values, social identities, moral foundations and attitudes is just as important as policy formulation. The social world plays a huge role in determining how ideas are acquired. Policy devotees need to understand that no one construct means exactly the same thing to everyone, as we will see.

So why do policies matter? First and foremost, because they affect people's lives. Good government policy can transform a society and save lives; bad government policy can have the opposite effect. Arguably, policies matter more to the new working class than they do to those who are better off: they are more likely to be reliant on state infrastructure and less likely to be able to move and compete in a globalised world than their better-off counterparts. However, due to political and economic imbalances of power, members of the new working class are less likely to have experienced policy decisions in their favour. The writer David Goodhart argues that the priorities of poorer Britons have been ignored compared to the dominant interests of the British elites,[2] whom he describes as the 'anywhere' grouping, the winners of three decades of social and economic liberalism.

To an extent, voters do assess the policies of the political parties on offer from the perspective of their interests. While the degree to which voters make a rational choice about who best will enact their preferences can overlook the multiple factors that influence party or candidate selection, sometimes policies will attract support based on having a direct positive (or negative) effect on the voter. For example, some young aspiring homeowners will have voted Conservative in 2015 to take advantage of the Help to Buy scheme; and there is no doubt that Theresa May's decision to include property value in the means test for adult social care (the so-called 'dementia tax') cost the Conservatives votes in the general election two years later. Equally, many students, and their parents, will have been drawn to the Labour Party's pledge to abolish tuition fees during the same election. Voters may express cynicism about so-called 'retail' policies, but parties need to offer the electorate attractive policies. As well as the material impact of these particular policies being relevant to voters, so, too, are their symbolic power – in two cases, triggering the association with the home – by giving them important 'clues' as to who the parties are and what they stand for, a theme we return to later.

The electorate also appraise the past actions of parties in government, and how they feel about the incumbents' performance. The effect of policies enacted in practice – not just what is on offer during an election campaign – has a tangible impact on voter assessment and perceptions of the political choices. Therefore the policies have to not only be credible during the campaign but also deliverable in reality. Often this is a negative judgement of dissatisfaction with a policy or set of policies, but it makes the formation of legitimate, credible and actionable policies a constant endeavour for a governing party. The new working class should be considered no different in this regard than any other social grouping. Even the most informed voters do not make political choices based solely on policy preferences,[3] and studies in political communications have found that more knowledgeable citizens are actually more responsive to emotional appeals than the average voter.[4] There is little substance to the notion that the enlightened, better educated citizen can live up to the ideal of democratic theory. To a greater or lesser extent, the way we vote comes from social and political identities, partisanship, party performance, the character of political leaders, and policies. And our hearts and minds help determine how we make those choices.

While voter assessment of policy is not the primary driver of political behaviour, policies do matter to winning votes because of their symbolic power; because they have an impact that is then assessed by the electorate; and because social and economic interests play a role in how people vote. Policies may become even more important in politics as more voters choose a different party to the last time at a general election.[5] However, there is no clear path between policy and ballot paper, and this has been fundamentally misunderstood and enacted for the past two decades.

Since the mid-1990s, and until the vote to leave the EU, followed by the unexpected surge in support for Jeremy Corbyn's Labour Party at the 2017 General Election, the dominant narrative in British politics was about capturing the centre ground. This is where elections had been fought and won in 1997, 2001 and 2005, and put forward as the reason why Labour lost support under Gordon Brown and Ed Miliband by those within the Labour Party who argued that only a return to centre-ground politics could see Labour in government again. The battle for the centre meant a fixation on the 'middle', which in both ideological and class terms was a more nebulous construct than it seemed. While there is clearly merit in devising a policy programme designed to appeal to a large number of voters, the 'median voter theory', whereby parties appeal to the median distribution point of voter views, presupposes that there is an ideological spectrum on which all voters sit.

However, party members and politicians are far more likely to be ideological than the typical voter, for whom this model assumes ends up maximising their choices with little effort as the politicians compete to pick up votes that cluster in the centre. Most voters do not see issues or policies through an ideological lens, and cannot reliably identify policy positions on the left or the right of the ideological spectrum.[6] Some voters are conventionally left wing on some things – like the NHS – but conventionally right wing on other things – like crime. And the 'centre' is not fixed: analysis shows that the centre actually moves in the opposite direction to government policy.[7]

Social and political group identity continues to be fundamental to voter choice, and in *Democracy for realists*, Christopher Achen and Larry Bartels argue that generally issue positions derive from identity. Which is not to say voters are not making rational choices at the ballot box, but that social and psychological attachments to groups remain an important factor in determining political behaviour. Therefore policy strategists need to think less about how they go about selling particular policies, or assuming particular policies will be appealing according to social and economic interests, and more about how they tell a story about who the party or candidate is that resonates with the voters' social group identification. Policies then become part of that story, rather than the story in and of itself.

How policies are communicated

Just as there is no clear line between policy preference and votes, there is no clear line between messenger and receiver when policy-makers are communicating with voters. The social psychologist Jonathan Haidt argues in *The righteous mind*[8] that intuition and emotion is most people's first response, and strategic reasoning comes second. Reasoning serves human intuition, rather than the other way round, which is what a rational choice theorist might suggest. Facts do matter, but more because they back up pre-existing cognitive structures, also known as frames, which give facts meaning rather than because they are persuasive by themselves, according to the cognitive linguist George Lakoff.[9] Haidt argues that humans are often 'groupish' rather than selfish in moral and political matters, as Lakoff also argues when he says humans tend to vote on values rather than self-interest, pointing out that those on low incomes will often vote against their economic self-interest to back conservative values. Humans deploy their reasoning skills to support their team and to demonstrate commitment to their team, according to Haidt. None of this means that policies are obsolete; far from it. But if the principles laid out by Haidt and Lakoff apply to politics, it means that policy persuaders need to stop looking blankly at the electorate when they don't buy the policy's rationale, and start tuning in to their values, social group identities and cognitive frames if they hope to be heard.

Pre-existing favourability of the political party or politician also matters to whether or not the policy substance can be received. Haidt says that when humans want to believe something, they ask 'Can I believe it?', but ask 'Must I believe it?' when they don't, and almost always answer 'yes' to the first question and 'no' to the second. In the mind of the voter, the standing and reputation of the message sender, which has typically been a party, or a candidate, or mainstream media, shapes whether or not a voter trusts and is willing to listen to them and their message. In some circumstances, voters undergo 'cognitive balancing' to adjust their preferences to adopt the favoured party's position. Both Labour and the Conservative parties have gone through significant periods where their tarnished brands have made it almost impossible for them to be heard by a sceptical electorate. For all of the 1980s, the Labour Party struggled to restore its electoral credibility, with negative voter recollection of their last period in government compounding an image that was off-putting to many. The Conservatives spent most of the Labour government years trying to rehabilitate their image as the 'nasty party', ironically a label given to them by their future leader, Theresa May.

'I don't engage with the news; if it comes on the radio I'll flick past it. I don't read it online or watch it on TV – Facebook is where I get most of my news from. I avoid it as it doesn't matter to me, it's not

> relevant to my life. I read books but not newspapers,
> sometimes I may use Twitter.' (Voter, Clacton-on-Sea)

Increasingly, voters' engagement in political debate is less filtered by mainstream media, as social media has become a much more significant feature of British political life. During the 2015 General Election, half of adult British social media users undertook some political activity on social media, a greater proportion than those reporting political activity offline.[10] For 'policy senders' this means that their messages and materials have to be shared peer-to-peer to be successful, as while the established channels and digital platforms try to navigate social media, it is much less easy to centrally control than traditional media. The first outstanding example of a politician in a mature democracy harnessing the power of the internet was Barack Obama during his campaign for Democrat Party nominee and then for US President, who capitalised on the ability that digital networks have to bring about new social formations.

Generally speaking, the rest of the political parties are playing catch up with a phenomenon that has outpaced traditional political techniques. During the 2017 General Election campaign, the Conservatives are thought to have spent £1 million on paid adverts on Facebook, YouTube and Twitter attacking Jeremy Corbyn, and while one received 9 million views on Facebook and YouTube, its repetitive 'attack' style failed to engage users. Labour's Momentum network of 20,000 campaigners in local groups focused on sharing videos through friends and family, which brought 2.4 times more traffic to Labour's website in the last month of the campaign than the Conservatives'.[11] Today, the senders of policy messages are likely to be someone voters have connected with online, a friend, family member or associate, rather than political commentators or the parties themselves. This has profound implications for parties needing to build trust and a network of messengers right across the social identity groupings of their electorate. It also makes the task of reaching out beyond traditional bases all the more important. Social media can reinforce 'group think' as users and platforms steer content the individual is likely to favour, reinforcing social exclusivity among voters. Public attitudes-led policy-making, outlined later in Chapter 7 on democracy, can offer a way of more objectively connecting with different groups alongside civic engagement.

Political strategists have long pointed out that there is a huge gap between what political parties think they are communicating and what people remember. Effective policy communication, where the target electorate receive and understand what is being fired at them from a political party, is pretty rare. Pollster Deborah Mattinson describes that by halfway through the 1997 General Election campaign, voters in focus groups could identify all five of the Labour Party's pledge card key policies.[12] In contrast, she says that voters in the marginal constituency of Harlow during the 2010 General Election couldn't recall any specific policies or pledges by the Conservatives to help them define the change in party brand that David Cameron had based his leadership on.[13] Her polling consultancy BritainThinks reported that during the 2017 General Election campaign only a handful of policies from any of the parties proved memorable. The most mentioned policies from voters in the seats surveyed for each party were the social care U-turn (Conservatives); abolishing tuition fees (Labour); and the decriminalisation of cannabis (Liberal Democrats).[14] BritainThinks also found that issues were most likely to cut through to the public when they confirmed existing views, for example, Labour as 'chaotic', for Shadow Home Secretary Diane Abbott's failure to recall the costs for a proposed policing policy, and the Conservatives as 'posh', for advocating for the reintroduction of fox hunting.

In common with political scientists, Mattinson concludes that most people do not follow politics closely, and find conventional politics boring and confusing. People are busy, and politics doesn't play a central role in most people's lives. There have been moments of peaked public interest, but these have tended to be political events that have gone against the grain, such as the independence referendum in Scotland or the EU referendum. The traditional party political broadcast has become less significant, and even in the month prior to the 2017 General Election, received a 0.06 per cent audience share compared to 16.29 per cent audience share for drama, 15.44 per cent for entertainment, and 14.27 per cent for documentaries. News programming, fiercely sought after by politicians, received just a 9.71 per cent audience share.[15] In 2017 only 3.5 million people watched the leaders' debate compared to 9.4 million for the first leaders' debate in 2010.[16]

Political parties wanting to showcase the fruits of policy advisers' labours are not just competing against one another but against a 24/7 world of instant engagement where people get to participate, and are not just on the receiving end of messages. Arguably politics has been one of the slowest industries to understand how digital technologies have changed people's expectations, and politicians who simply deploy old communications strategies in a digital world risk losing ground. Haidt points out that the more Western, educated, industrial, rich and democratic, the more the world is perceived as full of separate objects rather than relationships, therefore the rise of digital politics should be considered as, if not more, relevant to engaging with groups within the new working class. For many of those using newer technologies, this is fundamentally a social world, where the individual is an actor connected to others. Stories, brands and peers will matter more to political parties in the future than a receptive print media. In the context of winning elections, policies still count, but must be part of a story about who that party is and who is advocating for it.

Values of the new working class

Is there a distinct set of values for the new working class, and is class even relevant to values? Values are defined in this context as the beliefs and ideals of society that are desirable or undesirable in the eyes of the electorate. These are more constant over time than policy preferences. This book argues that there are values that are deeply ingrained in British society and that cut across class that all politicians would do well to understand.

However, there are subtle but important value differences to the new working class that political leaders have picked up on, but have clumsily expressed. This has largely been a reaction to the over-emphasis of the values of the dominant political class during the last two decades, which has overlooked important components of the beliefs and ideals of the new working class. Social class is still relevant to how people view social and political issues, but it depends on the topic as to whether it is the determinant factor. In some key areas, particularly economic issues, class experience still shapes political views.[17] In other areas, such as social equality, views are more likely to be shaped by education.

It is also important that politicians and communicators treat values as worthy of serious investigation and consideration as they do individual policies. Treating values glibly can result in generalisations, stereotyping, divisiveness and alienating voters if misunderstood or miscommunicated. This is particularly important as the dividing lines on class tend to be cultural rather than ideological, according to pollster Peter Kellner,[18] whose analysis says that while social class no longer affects votes as much as it used to, its influence is far greater than conventional polls suggest.

Research by YouGov revealed that the values that voters rate highest across all social classes in Britain today are 'family', 'fairness', 'hard work' and 'decency', followed by 'equality' and 'freedom'.[19] The first four values could be described as those deployed by Margaret Thatcher to galvanise the 'great middle mass' of British society, which were claimed as sectional, but ones that the academics Jon Lawrence and Florence Sutcliffe-Braithwaite describe as 'near-universal values rooted deep in the national psyche.'[20] They suggest that 'a diffuse, mutable language of 'ordinariness', hard-working respectability and family-centred individualism was mobilised to describe these people' to avoid potentially divisive class antagonisms.

The YouGov values research shows that while there are differences in emphasis across social classes, these don't correlate in line with class, and these top four values rank as most important for all classes (by occupational status, rather than subjective class status). For example, 'family' is seen as most important by occupational social grades C1s, C2s, E[21] (manual workers and those on low incomes; see the endnote for a detailed explanation of occupational social grades), equally as important as 'fairness' for Bs, and third to 'hard work' and 'fairness' by Ds. 'Hard work' is seen as less important to social class E than 'equality' and 'freedom'. 'Independence' is seen as more important to social class A than 'self-reliance' and 'freedom'. As a value, 'morality'

Figure 5: Rating values, by social class

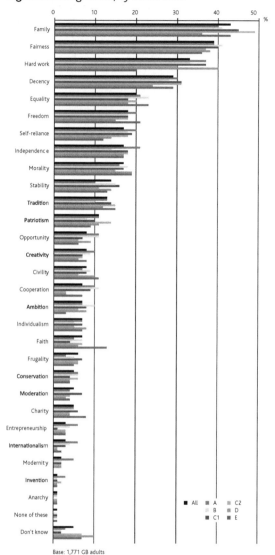

Base: 1,771 GB adults

Grade	Chief social class	Chief income earner's occupation
A	Upper middle class	Higher managerial, administrative or professional
B	Middle class	Intermediate managerial, administrative or professional
C1	Lower middle class	Supervisory or clerical and junior managerial, administrative or professional
C2	Skilled working class	Skilled manual workers
D	Working class	Semi-skilled and unskilled manual workers
E	Non-working	Casual or lowest grade workers, pensioners, and others who depend on the welfare state for their income

Source: Frayne (2015)

is described as more important to social classes D and E than it is to other classes; and 'faith' is seen as more important to social class E than any of the other classes. In Scotland, 'fairness' is rated the top value, followed by the same values as the rest of Britain: 'family', 'hard work' and 'decency'.

> 'My children are always my priority. You know. Do anything for them. Well, yeah, there's times me and Lisa have gone without a dinner so they could have dinner, you know.' (Voter, London)

The values voters most closely associate with the Labour Party are 'equality', 'fairness' and 'family' followed by 'hard work' and 'cooperation'. 'Cooperation' was not a value that scored particularly highly among the wider public. Three of the four values most closely associated with the Conservatives – 'entrepreneurship', 'tradition' and 'ambition' – do not appear in the public's top values. This suggests that Labour's perceived value base is more in tune with voter values than the Conservatives', which come across as narrower in appeal, right across the social classes. Conservative values tend to be more closely associated with economic success (for example, 'entrepreneurship' and 'ambition'), which the data shows are of less relative importance from the perspective of values, although matters of the economy and incomes from a policy and personal perspective are highly important during election campaigns.

The subsequent chapters review attitudes towards issues by income and class, and the policy options that may result, so this chapter will not discuss these differences in detail. However, there are particular political dividing lines that are worth noting. According to the academics Geoffrey Evans and James Tilley,[22] social class shapes what people think about fairness, the role of the state and how they define what is right or wrong. Attitudes by class to economic issues are less pronounced than they were, but Evans and Tilley suggest there is still a correlation that suggests that those more closely connected with the marketplace as employers and managers are more likely to support free market principles.[23]

Figure 6: Public values compared to those associated with Conservatives and Labour

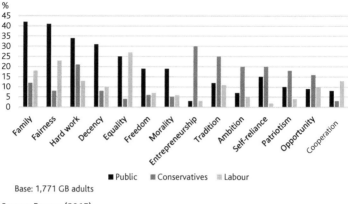

Base: 1,771 GB adults

Source: Frayne (2015)

The widest issues gap between the working and middle class is on immigration, where those who are in professional or managerial jobs are more likely to support migration from poorer countries than those who are in routine or semi-routine jobs.[24] Working-class voters and those on lower incomes generally are much more distrustful of MPs[25] and feel that they have less control over the issues that matter to them.[26] Particularly significant to this story is the finding that a majority of Britons of all classes feel that Britain has changed for the worse over the past 20-30 years, with 68 per cent of working-class people agreeing with that statement, and only 22 per cent tending to disagree, compared to 52 per cent of middle-class people.[27]

Triggering 'moral foundations'

Ever since the 1992 presidential campaign for Bill Clinton popularised the phrase 'It's the economy, stupid', it has been political wisdom that voters' belief in which party or leader triumphs on the economy will determine the election outcome. There is some truth in this, and a direct correlation between the performance of the economy in the run-up to the election and the effect on the incumbents. Yet this was either not entirely true then, or has become just slightly less important over time, as voters' cultural needs and emotional responses have come more to the fore. This was most evident during the campaign for the UK to remain in the EU, when warnings from 'Project Fear' about the supposedly dire economic consequences of a vote to leave the EU failed to cut through to an electorate that either did not believe the claims or did not prioritise them above other social, cultural and political considerations such as sovereignty. The fact that the famous claim of the Leave campaign that the NHS could receive £350 million more each week if the UK wasn't in the EU was discredited shortly after the vote with little backlash from Leave voters suggests that economic considerations were not the primary drivers of the vote.

'Rich people may not worry about money but they're still not happy, we need more than money to be happy.' (Voter, Birmingham)

In reality, social identities, perceived self-interest and values interact in voter behaviour, and there isn't always a neat pattern to explain why and how. Political parties understand that they need to trigger the right kind of emotions in voters, but do not always demonstrate that they know how to do so. A reasonable starting point would be voter values, and framing party values and policies aligned to the voter base. But to go deeper into connecting with voters' emotions requires understanding the moral positions underpinning their emotional response. If it is accepted that reason follows emotion, George Lakoff and Elisabeth Wehling[28] argue that every political argument should start with what is morally right or wrong policy-making on an issue. Morality is a difficult terrain for politicians, and let's face it, for most people. Each of us has our own version of moral truth, and Haidt points out that it is very difficult to consider that there might be more than one version of moral truth. Yet, he argues, this is exactly where politicians need to start.

One way to develop a strategic deployment of emotions in politics is to use Haidt's moral foundations theory.[29] Just as we have five taste receptors, Haidt notes that we have at least six innate moral foundations that help guide our emotional responses. Haidt argues that this is particularly important for the political left to grasp, as it has traditionally relied on a narrow set of moral foundations compared to the political right, who tend to be more comfortable associating with the full range of intuitions. For example, Lakoff and Wehling say that with the exception of Barack Obama in 2008, US Democrats do not promote their moral worldview enough, while Republicans since Reagan have been far more at ease openly talking about their values and politics as 'family life'. Haidt's six moral foundations are: *care* (the opposite of which is *harm*), which is about being sensitive to need. *Fairness* (the opposite of which is *cheating*) is about the rewards of cooperation without being exploited. *Loyalty* (the opposite of which is *betrayal*) is about trust and rewarding team players, ostracising or even killing those who betray the team. *Authority* (the opposite of which is *subversion*) is being sensitive to rank and status. *Sanctity* (the opposite of which is *degradation*) is investing objects with values to bind a group together (or to set it apart from others). And *liberty* (the opposite of which is *oppression*) resists attempted domination. Political strategists can draw on this moral foundations theory to enable them to understand why people might think differently, and to encourage them to activate the full set of receptors.

The new working class are just as intuition-driven as any other social grouping, and therefore any serious strategy designed to maximise voter support needs to offer clues to the electorate that activate different elements of the moral foundations theory. Symbolic policies[30] are a key tool to deploy, but strategists need to be aware of how the wrong foundations can be alerted, for example, if the party is aiming to engage the care foundation on welfare policy, but in the minds of voters, activates the cheating aspect of the fairness foundation. Lakoff and Wehling say that politicians and the media need to become much more conscious of the 'containers' they use to convey meaning, because humans have no access to realities outside of their perceptions. Therefore understanding which containers (metaphors) activate the desired meaning and which ones inadvertently evoke the frames of the opponent becomes central to political communication. Potential policies to activate the moral foundations will be drawn out throughout the course of subsequent chapters, and a new policy agenda is summarised in the book's concluding chapter, using voter values as the conceptual framework.

Social identities of the new working class

In the old politics of class, social groupings were more straightforward. In the days when the working class was politically organised in the form of trade unions, easy to address as a mass in factories, and would respond to the term 'working class', democratic representation and communication had a more linear path. Today, any party wanting to appeal to the new working class needs to have a first-hand understanding of the demographics, affiliations and identities of the diverse peoples who comprise this large constituency. As previously noted, the fact that this group doesn't identify as a coherent whole doesn't mean it doesn't exist, but it cannot be tidied into a convenient identity group. Rather, its composite social identities need to be understood and their desire to align with appropriate coalitions of social groupings. As the divisions between social class have become more blurred, so, too, have the groupings, but there is no going backwards to an era of mass collective identity. Group formation has been fundamentally altered by economic change and also by technological change, where new social networks are constantly being created around issues and shared interests, which transcend traditional boundaries and resist institutional direction.

The Conservative Party understand the need to expand their social identity base well. Broadly speaking, their voters tend to be older, more likely to be ethnically White, and better off. Yet despite winning the most votes at the last three general elections, projected demographics may not work in their favour. Every age group under 50 voted by a majority for Labour at the 2017 General Election, bringing the age at which a voter is more likely to vote Conservative than Labour to 47, up from 34 at the start of the campaign.[31] By 2050, one-third of the British population is expected to be non-White, and despite targeted interventions with particular minority ethnic groups, the Conservatives' vote among minority ethnic groups dropped in 2017, and Labour took 73 per cent of the minority ethnic vote.[32] Labour's efforts to court the younger voter in the run-up to the 2017 General Election, which were considered to be unlikely to produce a sufficient electoral return due to the relatively lower turn-out among young people, was a decisive factor in their increased vote share. The SNP has changed the political landscape in Scotland by activating a frame of national identity against the hostile grouping of the 'Westminster elite' (rather than the English as a people).

Even if these trends continue, the parties may well fare better than they expect on the basis of the past couple of elections. But while our society has become more individualised in many ways, and there is a declining proportion of party loyal voters and an increased proportion of floating voters, it is worth remembering that humans remain stubbornly 'groupish'. Relatively few constituencies change parties during any one election, and the basis of most people's political loyalties tend to be acquired early in life. Despite a cynical dismissal of young people's lack of overt collective affiliations, there is as yet no clear evidence to suggest that millennials (those born after 1980 and voting in their first general elections) are more individualised in their voting behaviour. The bigger issue in addressing the needs of young people is that their policy priorities are markedly different from the older generation, and political methods look pretty antiquated to the smartphone generation.

Engaging in a discussion about morals, values and attitudes is uncomfortable territory for many politicians, and requires considerable skill to do so effectively. But it is becoming increasingly essential. Across Europe, populist parties are gaining support, based on a national identity politics that emphasises socially conservative traditional values and hostility to foreigners. Matthew Goodwin argues that the rise in support of popular nationalism is fuelled by identity issues more than economic or material concerns, and says that 'as long as progressives fail to address the values gap, populists will have significant influence on Europe's political landscape.'[33]

'There's no nativity plays now and I do think that's unfair, because obviously it is a British country.' (Voter, London)

While Britain doesn't have the same levels of nationalist party support as Austria, France or Germany, some of the conditions for the rise in populist politics in the continent and in Donald Trump's victory in the US are evident in Britain, such as a tension between social liberalism and social conservatism. This plays out on a daily basis in the popular media that fuels, but also reflects, a low but significant level of resistance to the implementation of socially liberal values. Populists have an answer to this by stoking national identity politics, but this is hugely problematic as, by its nature, it requires definition of a people against 'others'. This book argues for an alternative proposition that is rooted in the public's core values of family, fairness, hard work and decency. British national identity does have an important role to play, but it needs to reflect the nation as we are – pluralist, multi-ethnic, tolerant and inclusive – particularly when policies are activated to encourage contribution and integration.

For politicians and parties seeking to engender groupish affiliation, the answer lies in democracy – first, in understanding the demographics, groupings, values and people within particular social identities. In many ways this is easier with the new working class than it is with the middle class, as they are more likely to be members of clubs and groups, slightly more likely to be part of a faith group and more likely to use community and public services. National parties need to understand the detrimental impact that alienating any one social identity grouping can have on their long-term prospects of building trust. For example, a poll for the think tank British Future found only a fifth of Black voters likely to vote Conservative in 2015,[34] and a separate poll found that just 13 per cent of Jewish voters were likely to vote Labour in the 2017 General Election, after a series of controversies about the party's handling of alleged anti-semitism.[35]

The most potent social identity is, of course, the family, which these days trumps the individual as a useful frame. Even if politicians have exhausted the rhetoric, they would do well to remember that women are more likely to see policy through the prism of their children's lives, their parents and their friends, and are 10 times more likely to refer to people when making their points about issues.[36] At a local level, there is no substitute for broad-based political activism to reach out to existing and new groups, place by place, so that the carriers of the message identify both with the party and with relevant social groupings.

Second, political parties need to effectively identify and communicate policy signifiers that help tell the new working class that they are on their side. This doesn't have to be at the expense of another group – class warfare is dead as a narrative, as it doesn't resonate for people, and parties need to bridge divides to get elected – but it does have to speak to their concerns. The single best example of this, in symbolic terms at least, is Thatcher's policy of council tenants gaining the 'right to buy' their council home. Policies should activate resonant moral foundations across the full suite, prioritising symbolic policies that are memorable and tell the voter who the party or leader is. Politicians need to think about what their values 'promise' is to voters in the same way that a successful brand would, and ensure that the experience of the policy delivers on it.

Third, the party has to look, feel and sound like the voters it is trying to associate with. Humans have a strong tendency to align with those of shared characteristics, and as we have seen in this chapter, to most citizens, this will be understood in social identity terms rather than as ideological frameworks. The traditional working class in particular has suffered a steep decline in visible political representation, with less than 10 per cent of MPs having previously done a working-class job before entering Parliament compared with a third of MPs in 1985.[37] Political parties have put resources into boosting their representations among under-represented groups, largely in recognition of the electoral imperative, but as social groups in Britain become more diverse, this becomes even more a question of political survival.

Policies do matter, but they need to be understood in the context of the relationship between the voter and the party or leader. Parties need to see the voters as if they were courting them for marriage – getting to know their friends and family, their interests and tastes, before they can secure their trust and be forgiven for not getting everything right. Policies, therefore, are like dates with someone you really want to like you: you might only get one shot, and a bad experience can be totally off-putting.

In the following chapters the book explores the social and political attitudes of the new working class towards the key areas that matter to them: families, education and health; the economy, work and welfare; homes, immigration and crime; and democracy. Attitudinal data is used to assess the policy options, and recommendations made for evidence-informed policies that speak to attitudes, values and activate the moral foundations of the new working class.

4

Families, education
and health

'I would love to better myself but it's very hard to do. [Friend] would love to go to university but it's very hard, will get a supermarket job and it's not what we want.' (Voter, Scarborough)

Politicians should not just introduce policies because public support indicates that they would be popular, nor avoid policies just because there is no public support. But starting with what the public think – and not just the new working class – does suggest what the priorities should be, what the public's views are, what the likely vote winners are, and demonstrates where ground needs to be laid for important but less popular policies. Policy is more likely to stick for the long term if there is the public will to support it,[1] therefore grounding policy-making in public opinion as well as evidence allows the public to see policies being implemented that reflect their concerns, in addition to offering them good value for money, because evidence suggests they are what will be effective. Policies have only been strongly recommended in this book where there is both public will and evidence pointing towards the policy, and divergence between public sentiment and evidence has been drawn out where it exists.

What are the issues that matter most to the new working class? Money and personal finances are the most commonly identified issues in public attitudes data, followed by health, immigration, caring for someone else, work and housing.[2] The topics covered in this book have been selected because they are the issues that score highly in public opinion polls as of concern to the new working class, as well as coming up as 'front of mind' issues when individuals are interviewed for qualitative research. The reason the reader will not find detailed discussion of foreign affairs or media regulation is simply because for most of the voters this book is concerned with, and arguably most voters in general, those issues are not their primary concerns.

There is a profound disconnect between the concerns of the new working class and the dominant political discourse as presented by the mainstream media. Even within a topic, the language and preoccupations of politicians, traditional policy experts and the media rarely reflect the language and preoccupations of the people on whose behalf they serve. It is like observing speakers of two different languages who have long since stopped trying to have a meaningful conversation: policy experts and politicians are doing the equivalent of speaking their own language more loudly, and wondering why the other person is looking perplexed.

The issues that matter to the new working class are not necessarily that different to voters in general – even topics that frequently present for the new working class such as health or

Figure 7: Six most frequent worries or concerns, according to income

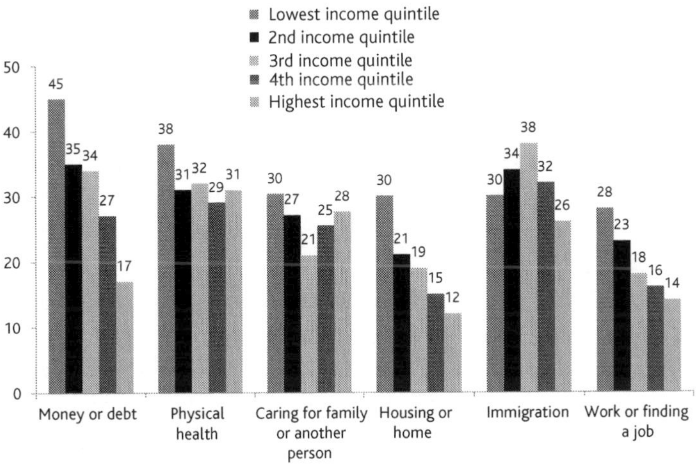

Source: Taylor et al (2017)

immigration are of concern right across the income and class spectrum. Targeting policies only on the things that speak to a voter's socioeconomic status will narrow political appeal, when the individual will have a more rounded range of considerations when they vote. This suggests that many of the policies that the new working class might need and respond to do not have to sit at odds with the needs and priorities of middle-class voters. From a political perspective, this makes building an alliance between those constituent parts of the electorate distinctly possible if the correct issues and policies are selected to promote. Interestingly, some policies favoured by the new working class are also favoured disproportionately by women, such as freezing energy bills, which further confirms the need for political parties to build alliances between the interests of differing and overlapping social identities to win a parliamentary majority.

The intention of this book is to amplify the views of the new working class and propose policies that speak to their concerns and interests. Using data from the British Social Attitudes (BSA) survey, cross-referenced with data from public opinion polling by YouGov and the National Centre for Social Research (NatCen), each thematic chapter that follows introduces the relative significance of the topic to the new working class, attitudes to the topic area (distinguishing whether the attitudes presented are by income, class and which definition, or for all public), and identifies the policies and ideas that would be most appealing to the new working class. On some issues there will be differences by class or income, but on others there will be little variation. It is also important to recognise that class and income are not always the dominant features that shape attitudes. Age, education, geography, ideological leaning (such as placement on authoritarian–libertarian or right–left scales) arguably plays as much or more of a role than class or income, depending on the issue. Starting with families and children, this first thematic chapter analyses attitudes data and policy responses on families, children, education, health and social care, drawing out policies to win the hearts, minds and votes of the new working class.

Families and children

Families and children are often the most important thing in people's lives. While as a social or political issue they do not present as highly as topics such as health or personal finance, families are the prism through which many voters assess policy. For example, voters say they mostly decide who to vote for based on what their policies will mean for them and for their family, and this is even more so the among those in occupational social classes C2DE[3] (manual workers and those on low incomes; see the endnote for a detailed explanation of occupational social grades[4]). Chapter 3 noted the finding that women are 10 times more likely to refer to people when making their points about issues, specifically their children, parents and friends.[5] It also found that 'family' is the highest scoring value among voters, followed by 'fairness', 'hard work' and 'decency'.[6] The BSA identifies that most people agree that 'watching children grow up is life's greatest joy', and this is even more the case for people on low incomes, 93 per cent of whom agree with this statement compared to 80 per cent on the highest incomes.[7] Caring for someone is the fourth most important concern for people on low to middle incomes, which could be a child, parent or another adult.[8] However, this attachment to family has been primarily adopted by politicians for its rhetorical power in deploying the term 'families' ('hard working', 'ordinary' or just 'working') in speeches, rather than presenting a sustained programme to strengthen families.

Families in Britain today have come a long way from the traditional unit of a usually male breadwinner and stay-at-home mother, and public attitudes have become much more accepting of different family formations. Remaining single and cohabiting has increased, marriage rates have declined and cohabiting couple families are the fastest growing family form in Britain.

Increasing ethnic diversity also has an impact on family formation: almost all mothers who are Bangladeshi, Pakistani or Indian are married when their child is born, compared with about 70 per cent of mothers who are White and just over half of mothers who are Black Caribbean.[9] Lone parents account for 2.8 million of the 19 million families in the UK,[10] and life is often particularly tough for those reliant on one income, especially in recent years, as costs have risen and incomes have flattened.

Changes to working life have fundamentally altered family life, with 3 million people now working night shifts,[11] and many workers travelling longer distances to their jobs because of relative housing costs. The increased participation of women in the labour market has necessitated changes to the world of work and to family life and childcare, and it is increasingly necessary for two parents to be earning to achieve a decent standard of living if neither is a top earner. The Joseph Rowntree Foundation estimates that a couple with two children need to have earnings of at least £20,400 each to achieve a socially acceptable minimum standard of living, and a lone parent with a preschool child needs £25,900.[12]

Family life is not just about income, but financial pressures for mid- to low-income groups place additional pressures on households that the state has a legitimate interest in, both for the personal impact on children and their parents, but also because of the lifetime social and economic consequences of childhood poverty.

> 'I wouldn't have changed anything. I think I've given them a lot of my time. I've organised my life around them, I think, but they've turned out great.... I'm happy with what I've done.' (Voter, Bristol)

Public attitudes to families and children

Family-friendly policies have undergone a significant transformation in the last 20 years, with the introduction of statutory paternity and increased maternity leave, flexible working and state contributions to preschool childcare. There is some public backing for extending state childcare support for parents, but it is not clear-cut. While the family and child-friendly policy that voters preferred in a YouGov/Policy Exchange poll was increasing the number of free childcare hours,[13] only around half of voters support this extension.[14] There is also limited support for the right to a year off work to care for a sick relative, and about half of voters support doubling paternity pay, according to an extensive survey for the Trades Union Congress (TUC) following the 2017 General Election.[15]

Arguably voters are being presented with a limited palette of options, but their equivocation acts as a barometer of the extent to which the taxpayer is willing to pay for goods they will not necessarily access. The policies that followed childcare in popularity among social grade C2DE voters were locating nurseries in primary schools where possible; extending the school day (although this was slightly less popular among this occupational class than among ABC1s); increasing statutory holiday entitlement (which was even more popular with ABC1s); and making tax-free savings for children more generous.[16] When it comes to social security spending, the public are generally supportive of more spending on parents who work on very low incomes (61 per cent[17]), although this has to be seen in the context of welfare spending overall.

Low- to middle-income parents say that finding the right kind of care to meet theirs and their child's needs, as well as awareness of their options, is a particular issue for them. Many report being unaware of the existing availability of state support as well as saying they would like more information. A study found that working-class parents felt that childcare was more inaccessible and expensive for them, and that there were not enough local childcare places available.[18] Because of the cost of childcare, many parents on lower and middle incomes would not earn more than the cost of the care even though they receive more state support, and also not benefit from the type of job flexibility enjoyed by many better-off parents. It is also important not to assume that all parents want state-funded childcare, as some want the choice to stay at home with their children when they are young. While state-subsidised childcare places may well serve as an important driver for getting mothers back to work after having children, it may be that from those mothers' perspectives, there is at least as much a need to invest in their skills as working adults.

'I've got my own aspirations and I want to do a job and for my son.... [cries]' (Voter, Scarborough)

There is a view that less well-off people hold more socially conservative views about the family than their better-off counterparts, and while there is some truth in this, which is also related to education levels, the differences have been somewhat overstated. For example, 60 per cent of people on low incomes think pre-marital sex is not at all wrong compared to a more liberal average of 75 per cent of the general public,[19] and 51 per cent of those on low incomes agree that 'housewives are central to the life of local communities in Britain' compared to 36 per cent of the highest income group.[20] While there is still a long way to go (for example, only 43 per cent of the public think it is acceptable for a police officer to be transgender, even though 84 per cent say they are not prejudiced at all towards transgender people[21]), there is a long-term trend towards more socially liberal views among all groups. In any case, it is important to remember that the new working class constitutes a much broader range of views than what constituted the traditional working class, which only comprises 14 per cent of the population, according to the Great British Class Survey (GBCS) data.

Policies for families and children

The difficulty in combining the predominantly private sphere of family and politics is that translating pro-family sentiment into policy reality often lacks a robust evidence base (such as the marriage tax allowance) or comes across as though the politician espousing the policy would like to return to the 1950s. Family policy has become largely about childcare, partly because quality, availability and affordability are real issues for parents, but partly because it is a relatively safe win for politicians. However, a policy environment that prizes families getting together and staying together really matters to the prospects of children in low- to middle-income families as well as for their parents. Strong families able to withstand the shocks of personal change and external pressures such as job loss are vital, especially for those who haven't gone to university and need to navigate a changing working world where their skills can become rapidly outdated. In this first section on families, three policy areas have been chosen that speak to the priorities and values of the new working class, based on a review of attitudes and available evidence.

Many of the family-friendly policies that have been introduced over the past two decades have benefited workers already in stable employment. For example, to qualify for occupational maternity leave, most employers require women to have worked for the employer for a set period. However, for workers in much more precarious employment, not only do changing working patterns and insecure contracts mean they are less likely to benefit from existing family provision, but unpredictable and unsocial work can make maintaining stable family life much tougher. Fathers who work unsocial hours typically have 15 hours less a week with their children than those who work regular, social hours,[22] and over 1 million families in Britain have at least one parent working on both weekend days.[23] Employers in the UK are more likely than their European counterparts to regularly require their workers to work at weekends,[24] and most mothers who work weekends say they would prefer not to if they have a choice.[25] Policies developed by government or political parties need to speak to the reality of combining work and family life for the new working class, which means not assuming that there is a typical family unit based on their own experience.

Policy 1. Make families and family stability a central organising principle for government policy, backed by policies that support it, such as putting the 'Family Test' on to a statutory footing. There is currently limited support for extending family policy as such, like family-friendly working, but government policy can have a destabilising effect on low- to middle-income families in particular, and therefore policy on housing, tax, health or welfare should routinely assess the impact on families. Former Prime Minister David Cameron introduced a 'Family Test' for government departments, but a review one year on found that a majority of government departments had shown limited commitment to implementing it.[26] The Family Test is unlikely to be a pledge card-style vote winner, and could be backed with a more symbolic policy such as an additional bank holiday to bring the UK up to the European average, or guaranteeing time off for families who work weekends. 'Family time' policies would demonstrate that the party was listening to the concerns and interests of low- to middle-income voters, for whom some of the welcome parental rights may have passed by.

Raising children when parents are on a low income can be stressful for the whole family. While there is not widespread public support for ramping up levels of social security to the point that would guarantee families had state support to reach a decent standard of living, there is some backing for increasing spending on families and children,[27] and the vast majority of the public recognise that there is child poverty in Britain.[28] Family incomes are partly in the control of the families themselves and their earnings, but the state does play a role for low- to middle-income families in providing support, and some of the recent changes in government policy have reduced incomes for some groups (caps and freezes on many working-age benefits and cuts to Work Allowance and other entitlements in Universal Credit, which is being slowly rolled out over the coming years).

There is a trade-off between ensuring that tax and benefits policy does not push families into poverty, incentivising parents to work when they can, and public legitimacy for limits to social security spending. However, the BSA survey suggests that public opinion may have reached a tipping point, and that cuts have gone far enough. It is also worth remembering that at the same time that some families reliant on state support will become worse off as a result of policy changes, the government has introduced a marriage tax allowance for all couples regardless of whether they have children, and increased the personal tax allowance. This benefits some low-income households, but in the main, it benefits those on middle to higher incomes when they would probably not be expecting a tax cut during such austere times. At the very least, families who are struggling to make ends meet should not have life made even tougher by cuts to state support.

Policy 2. Safeguard family incomes by reversing cuts to families reliant on benefits and tax credits. Families are falling further behind a decent standard of living, and even with increases to the National Minimum Wage, work does not necessarily provide financial security. Increases to the personal tax allowance could be made available only to those with children under 18,[29] either directly through a new tax allowance or via targeted family income support. A policy aimed at incentivising marriage (such as the marriage tax allowance) should be reformed to focus on families with children rather than financially rewarding marriage as an act, and be extended to cohabiting couples with children to encourage family formation and stability.

Parental involvement has a known impact on children's learning, and there are steps the state can take to encourage involvement, particularly when it is likely to have most impact, which is considered to be in the early, preschool years.[30] Reading to a child at age 5 makes a positive difference to their test scores at age 11, although it has less of an effect during the school years, indicating that early involvement is particularly important.[31] Once young children are out of the supervision of health visitors, there is a long period of little state interaction for new parents. Access to affordable and high-quality preschool care for children matters to parents, both for their children and for their peace of mind if they are considering returning to work. Political parties could have a serious win by seeing preschool years as the early opportunity to increase parental involvement in improving children's longer-term outcomes once at school, providing working parents with links to improving their own education, and enabling parents to return to work.

Policy 3. Set up a new state-backed guarantee on early years to increase parental involvement in children's education and to increase opportunity for parents. Preschool education is a chance to bed in parental involvement and give children a good start, particularly with reading and writing. The present funding arrangements are poorly targeted and understood by low-income parents. They could be better orientated towards a clearer offer of higher quality provision (state, voluntary or private) if linked to children's outcomes, and integrated into schools where possible to deliver early literacy and related family support. The Social Market Foundation recommends funding schools to increase support for parents in helping children to read by running after-school literacy classes for parents and pupils together, and launching a programme of after-school 'family literacy' classes in primary schools targeted at areas with higher levels of deprivation.[32]

Education

Education enjoys strong support from the general public, and along with health, features as their top area for increased government spending.[33] Whether or not they have children, 71 per cent of the public support much more spending on education. This has risen as an issue of concern to voters since 2010, and jumped in 2016-17. In Ipsos MORI's *Issues Monitor* of May 2017 [34] it came third to health and Brexit in the important issues to voters, overtaking immigration. This rise is replicated in Scotland, where the proportion of Scottish voters choosing improving standards of education when asked what the Scottish Government's highest priority should be increased from 12 per cent in 2007 to 22 per cent in 2015.[35] Among low-income voters, 30 per cent of participants in a NatCen panel survey identified education as an important 'front of mind' issue,[36] and naturally enough were more likely to choose education if there were children in the household. For people on low to middle incomes, education features as one of the issues of concern, after health, immigration, money or debt, and work. People are significantly more likely to think they can't do anything to improve their education situation compared to their health, work or money situation.[37]

Education, and more precisely, graduating from university, has a strong correlation with social class. Just 4 per cent of the GBCS' precariat class has a university degree, compared with 56 per cent of the elite and 40 per cent of the established middle class. Only 11 per cent of the traditional working class and 18 per cent of the emerging service workers have a degree, probably reflecting their lower average age of 32 given that higher education has expanded rapidly in the last two decades (compared to the average age of 66 for a member of the traditional working class and 50 for the precariat). Higher numbers of working-class young people have gone to university in this time, but not nearly so many as their middle-class counterparts, who have benefited disproportionately from investment in higher education, just as disinvestment in further and technical education has had a disproportionate impact on the prospects of non-university graduates.

Public attitudes to education

Public opinion is clear about expectations from the education system. Eighty-four per cent of the general public say turning out confident and self-assured young adults is very important, followed by pupils going on to find fulfilling employment (80 per cent).[38] Academic success is seen as important, but not as important as work readiness or social development, with 68 per cent saying it is very important that pupils make good progress no matter their starting point, and only 22 per cent saying it is very important a high proportion go on to university. Even if the public want schools to prepare young people well for work, only around half the population think secondary schools do so, and people who are unemployed are less likely to think they do.[39] A strong majority think it is more difficult for young people to get a job now than it was when they completed their full-time education.[40] Despite this, there is little support for increased government spending on benefits in relation to school leavers. All groups support the role of schools in developing the skills and knowledge to get a good job and rate this above gaining qualifications and certificates, although both functions receive strong public support.

Despite recent political debate centring on the planned expansion of grammar schools and academies, the public is much less certain that those structures deliver the outcomes they want. Grammar schools are perceived as only slightly better than secondary modern schools, the alternative for children who do not go to a grammar school, in turning out confident and self-assured young adults (61 per cent compared to 58 per cent).[41] They are considered no better at preparing pupils for fulfilling employment. Around 61 per cent of the public oppose selection for secondary schools, although a significant minority support selection,[42] which currently only represents about 5 per cent of the state sector (around 7.3 per cent of children are privately educated). NatCen found that there was more support for educational selection among older, male, Conservative-supporting voters in London, the South East, East and North West, and attitudes were associated with the type of school

Figure 8: What do the public want from the education system?

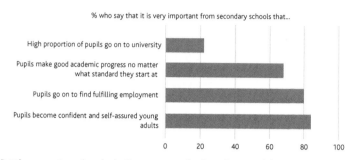

% who say that it is very important from secondary schools that...

But they are not convinced selective grammar schools are better at delivering the characteristics they consider most important ...

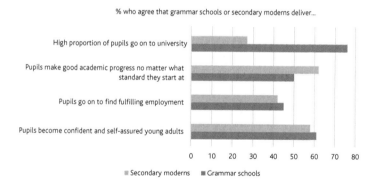

% who agree that grammar schools or secondary moderns deliver...

And academies are not expected to improve schools either ...

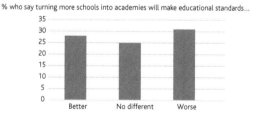

% who say turning more schools into academies will make educational standards...

Source: Tanner and Kelley (2017); Dahlgreen (2016) on academies

the respondent went to. About half of the public (53 per cent) support an expansion of grammar schools.[43] Over half the public (56 per cent) say turning schools into academies will either make no difference to educational standards or worsen them, compared to 28 per cent who say it will improve educational standards.[44] Support for academies has dropped from 40 per cent in 2011 to 25 per cent in 2016.[45]

Another prominent education policy has been the introduction of free school meals during the first three years of primary school.[46] Around half of the public support the policy, and support is strongest among C2DE voters, but over a third think the money would be better spent elsewhere.[47] Around 60 per cent of voters were found to support the policy of extending free school meals to all children paid for by removing the tax exemption on private schools,[48] a policy contained in the 2017 Labour Party manifesto. There was little support for introducing free school breakfasts and going back to only children on low incomes receiving free school lunches. Reversing school funding cuts (spending has increased, but not in per pupil terms) and ensuring schools have the resources they need was supported by around half of voters.

A separate YouGov poll found voters favoured introducing stricter discipline in schools as their top policy priority, followed by reducing class sizes, and making sure exam standards match the best in the world.[49] Improving vocational education came next for C2DE voters, along with spending more time teaching maths and science, and then spending more time teaching advanced IT skills like coding and programming. There is also support for parents being allowed to take children out of school during term time for family holidays, and this is slightly more strongly supported by C2DE voters.[50]

Despite Labour's electoral success with young people for its pledge to scrap tuition fees in its 2017 manifesto, a vast majority of the public support charging most students some kind of fees for higher education.[51] A consistent two-thirds support some students or their families paying fees, around one in ten support charging all students, and one in five oppose all fees. Only around a quarter favour maintenance grants for everyone, and opinion is divided on whether students should take out loans while studying.

There is also a level of scepticism about the value of higher education, with almost all groups saying they did not think that a university degree represented good value for money, and this is particularly true of younger voters.[52] There has been a huge expansion of higher education in recent decades, and while 43 per cent of the public think there are too many graduates in the market, only 12 per cent support reducing places. While university tuition remains free in Scotland, there are almost identical attitudes in Scotland towards higher education as England and Wales. Given the £8.6 billion spent by the state on higher education,[53] and the average £50,000 debts of today's university graduates,[54] the government should be concerned regarding public cynicism about the rewards from that sizable expenditure.

Policies for education

It is quite clear from the public attitudes data that successive governments are well out of line with public opinion on education priorities. There is no clamour for grammar schools, academies or a return to universal free higher education, not among the general public or parents. Voters want a good education system that sets young people up for the future, but are not convinced they are getting it, or that universities are delivering it, and are also not convinced that the policy direction towards the expansion of academies and grammar schools is going to deliver it either. There is a strong and clear message from voters: stop meddling with school structures and focus on outcomes for young people.

From a policy perspective, there is concern that Britain's burgeoning higher education institutions are failing to fulfil the needs of employers, graduates or wider society. One in three graduates ends up in a non-graduate job, and there are universities where graduate earnings are no higher than non-graduates.[55] At the same time, the relative decline of technical and vocational options for young people who do not go to university has meant that there are limited opportunities at age 18 and beyond, as adults find themselves without the skills required in a fast-paced changing world of work. The problem is not confined to higher and further education. While funding per pupil in primary and secondary schools has doubled since the 1990s, the literacy and numeracy skills of 16- to 24-year-olds in the UK are among the worst in the developed world. Fewer than half of UK school children complete work placements, compared to 87 per cent in France.[56]

Social background continues to play a prominent role in educational outcomes, despite years of rhetoric of schools as an engine of social mobility: the single biggest predictor of age 11 attainment improvement since age 5 is household income.[57] There is little evidence that any of the current preoccupations of the major parties – academies and free schools, grammar schools, free university tuition fees for all or free school meals – will tackle any of the major challenges of the education system, and for the experience of pupils of the new working class in particular.

Policy 1. Re-focus education on lifetime outcomes, primarily finding and sustaining fulfilling employment in the future economy. Britain's employers have a major stake in educational outcomes, and should have a stronger role and responsibility to help equip schools to develop skills for the future, particularly given the major changes brought about by technology. Employers need to drive a much more ambitious British education system, able to meet the expectations the public has and the changing skills needs of the economy. The narrow choices presented to pupils at age 16 should be revisited, rather than fixating on how grades are designed. Young people need to be inspired and supported with high-quality careers advice and transitions to meaningful post-16 education and training that is more highly rewarded by society and the labour market.

'You're a product of your environment. Some of the schools around here are only interested in bums on seats; they don't have an expectation that you could go on to university. Being from around here means you are looked down on in the academic world.' (Voter, Port Talbot)

The ideal of education as a leveller between those born with privileges and those without is a myth, at least in the UK. The differences in attainment between those who are well off and those who are not are stark. A total of 36.5 per cent of children who are classified as the least well-off gain 5 A★-C GCSEs compared with 64 per cent of all other pupils, a gap of 27.4 percentage points.[58] Inequalities at birth are exacerbated, not lessened, by the current UK education system, and despite serious investment, the large gap between the richest and poorest pupils has not shown significant improvement in the period between the 1980s and mid-2000s.[59] A child from a high-income, high-qualified household has an average test score at age 11 a remarkable 10 points higher than a child who has a parent with no qualifications.[60] From the perspective of the new working class, getting the very basics of education and schooling right is vital rather than the type of school structure, which has not produced convincing evidence that structures improve pupil outcomes more than other factors.

Policy 2. Focus on closing the educational attainment gap of low- to middle-income pupils, improving their educational and lifetime outcomes. There is solid evidence about what works: in short, getting the best teachers into schools with the highest levels of deprivation and ensuring that pupil premium funding is spent on best-evidenced practice to improve outcomes. Schools may need support to incentivise teachers to make costs like housing more affordable.[61] The Joseph Rowntree Foundation recommends evaluating trials aimed at attracting high-quality teachers and leaders where they are most needed.[62] Policies like reducing class sizes are popular with parents, and smaller class sizes can have a positive effect on attainment and behaviour, but this tends to be small and diminishes over time.[63] If public demand for a good school system that prepares young people well is to be met, high-quality teaching is the way to achieve it.

While university expansion has been positioned as a great opportunity for working-class children to access institutions previously reserved for the offspring of the middle class, the reality tells a different story. Young people from the new working class need to have all the same opportunities as young people from any other background, yet expansion has inadvertently increased the gap between the middle class and the less advantaged. Universities, particularly the elite institutions that entrench privilege rather than build a genuine meritocracy, need to be put under far more stringent scrutiny and consequences if they do not rapidly increase access for working-class and minority ethnic young people. And while increasing access to a university education for those from worse-off backgrounds is right, a focus on universities alone will not bring about the kind of transformation the new working class requires, given the vastly unequal starting point. The focus for meaningful policy change should be a gradual shift towards further and vocational education and training, to increase the status of the associated professions and qualifications so that the consequences of not getting a university degree are less severe. The Institute for Government points out that further education, vocational and skills training has been subjected to 28 separate pieces of legislation since the 1980s and no organisation has lasted longer than a decade. Rachel Wolf, former adviser to former Prime Minister David Cameron, attributes this policy churn directly to the fact that journalists, politicians, their children and their friends are unlikely to have gone through further education themselves, and are therefore unlikely to notice that anything is wrong because they 'will not have friends who are experiencing disaster.'[64] At the same time, the economy needs a capable workforce trained and skilled to adapt to the jobs of the future, not just to meet today's labour market needs.

Policy 3. Establish a new generation of employer-backed skills and education institutes for young people and adults of working age, gradually shifting state resources from higher education to improve the lifetime outcomes from the education system. The regulator needs to play a more robust role in protecting the consumer to prevent poor quality courses being taught, and managed consequences for underperforming higher and further education institutions. The present situation brings all the downsides of a market-based approach, but without the potential benefits of sufficient improved quality. Employers need to work with government and schools locally to enhance non-graduate employment, workplace training and boost higher-quality, higher-skilled apprenticeships. Resources need to be directed to support the rollout of Technical Level qualifications if they are to be a success.

Health and social care

Health is a priority for people of all groups, and the NHS in particular is not just a political priority, but part of our national identity. Most Britons say the NHS is what makes them most proud to be British, more so than the armed forces, the Royal Family or the BBC.[65] The NHS is considered one of our proudest achievements, but the public is also worried about current pressures and its future. Across the population as a whole, concern about the NHS has been rising, reaching its highest level since 2002 in May 2017,[66] as well as the highest number of people since 2002 who expect it to get worse.[67] For those in the lowest income category, physical health is second only to debt or money worries. Mental health is also an issue in all income groups, although features more strongly in the lowest income group.[68] Caring for someone is slightly more of a concern for those in the lowest income group than for other income groups.[69]

There are particular features of the new working class that differentiate their health and care needs compared to the general population. While life expectancy has been generally rising, men and women in the lowest social class will, on average, live just over seven years less than those in the highest social class, and be more likely to live those years with a disability or longstanding illness.[70] Those who comprise the new working class are more likely to be in lower-wage jobs, and the majority of areas with persistently low life expectancy have a high proportion of people earning low or no wages.[71] While many will go on to higher-paid roles, only one in six workers on low wages will have escaped low wages 10 years later,[72] making their ability to save for a secure future virtually impossible. With a lower annual average income than their middle-class counterparts, they are more likely to need state support as they age. During their lifetimes, people who make up the new working class will be more likely to be caring for someone and more likely to have a disability themselves.[73] Those with poor mental health are more likely than those with physical conditions alone to be trapped in more precarious and low-paid work.[74] The health and support needs of the new working class will naturally vary, but the one thing they have in common is their vulnerability to increased costs over the lifetime relative to those with more wealth and income. And all of the major indicators of public health show that the gap in good health between the wealthiest and least well-off – from life expectancy to infant mortality to quality of life – is widening.[75]

> 'It's the grind that gets you down, every single day.... I think what contributes to me being ill was having so many years of having to cope, basically.' (Voter, Wiltshire)

Public attitudes to health and social care

Almost everyone in Britain supports government provision of healthcare, and this has been consistent over the last 30 years. Ninety-six per cent of voters agree that it is the government's responsibility to provide healthcare for the sick, and this is even higher in Scotland and Wales than in England.[76] Only 2 per cent disagree with the statement that the government should support an NHS that is tax-funded, free at the point of use, and provides comprehensive care for citizens.[77] There is strong support to maintain the principles of the NHS, and younger people are even more likely than older people to say that we must do everything we can to maintain the NHS.[78] Around 8 in 10 members of the public think the government should spend more or much more on health, even when reminded that this could mean higher taxes.[79] However, the public does not have an unlimited appetite for ever-increasing public spending on the NHS, and a majority are not willing to deprive other public services to maintain the NHS at its current levels.[80] In general, there are no strong differences in attitudes towards the NHS and social care by income or class.

Social care for older people and those with disabilities does not feature as prominently as a concern for the general public as healthcare,[81] probably reflecting the fact that fewer people have a need for or experience of it; however, people are much more dissatisfied with social care than with GPs, the NHS or dentists.[82] There are only small differences in levels of satisfaction with the NHS reported by income,[83] which is a change from a few years ago, when rates of dissatisfaction were generally higher, and those on a higher income were more likely to express dissatisfaction. However, in Scotland, those who are struggling on their present income (37 per cent compared with 21 per cent of those living comfortably on present income) were more likely to say they were dissatisfied with the standard of the NHS.[84] UKIP supporters are more likely than any other party supporters to express dissatisfaction with the NHS (32 per cent dissatisfied, compared to 18 per cent of Conservative supporters).[85] Today, people who are dissatisfied with the NHS are likely to relate this to resources and pressure on services, with 'waiting times' the most frequently cited answer followed by 'too few staff'.[86] For disabled people or those with ongoing health needs, the cost of prescriptions and changes to assessment for benefits are particular issues, and worry about the social stigma of being labelled welfare-dependent if social security payments are spent on visible items like a mobility scooter.[87]

Almost all the public recognise that the NHS has a funding problem, and support for addressing this through increasing tax has started to rise. When presented with the options for increasing NHS funding, 49 per cent support higher taxes, 20 per cent say the NHS should live within its budget, and 30 per cent support increasing charges for patients (such as for missed GP appointments or non-medical items like laundry in hospital).[88] This is a rise in public acceptability for paying more tax to increase NHS funding of 8 percentage points compared to the 2015 survey. More recently, in August 2017, research by Ipsos MORI for The King's Fund found that two-thirds of people would be willing to pay more in taxes to maintain current levels of care and services.[89]

There is some ambiguity on charging: when asked which charges they support, a majority support charging for missed appointments; there is some support for charging for procedures not deemed clinically necessary (but what that constitutes is unclear); but most people are opposed to charging for a guaranteed GP's appointment; and opinion is split on charging patients who have diseases and illnesses caused in some way by their lifestyle.[90] Reflecting the strong support for the founding principles of the NHS, there is little appetite for moving to an insurance system, and three-quarters support charging more for foreign visitors who use the NHS. There is little support for deviating from the principles of a universal system for citizens: 73 per cent oppose restricting the NHS to those on lower incomes.[91]

In a YouGov poll looking specifically at policy responses, the most popular policy based on the options provided was preventing foreign nationals coming to the UK just to use the NHS, followed by extending GP opening hours, reducing the cost of care homes and increasing the number of nurses in hospital wards.[92] Improving mental health was an area with particular support among those with an income of less than £10,000. There was also strong support for decisions about public services being made by professionals and experts rather than politicians, and for decisions to be taken locally to reflect the needs and priorities of local people.[93] A majority of the public say they believe people should be consulted on what treatments and services are available, but that the final decision should rest with professionals.[94]

Figure 9: Public support for funding the NHS

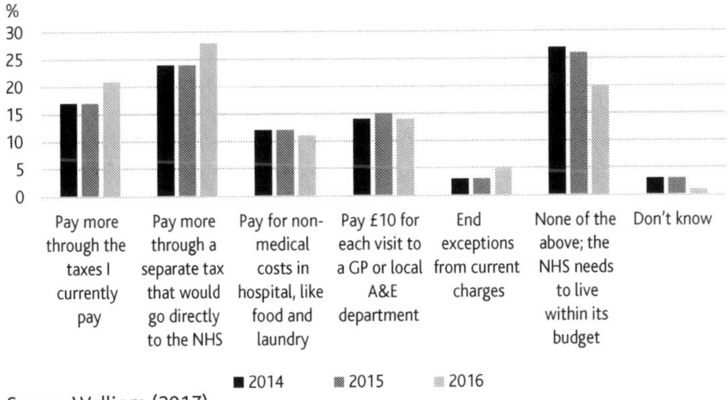

Source: Wellings (2017)

While there is almost universal support for the government to provide comprehensive healthcare free at the point of need, the public are less concerned with who delivers the service on the government's behalf. Forty-three per cent of the public say they do not have a preference about who delivers their NHS-funded treatment, while 39 per cent prefer their NHS-funded care to be delivered by an NHS organisation, and 16 per cent prefer a private service.[95] Of those who do express a preference, just over two-thirds say they would prefer NHS provision. People remain wary regarding privatisation of public services, with 60 per cent of all voters disagreeing that private companies should be allowed to play a bigger role in running state schools and NHS hospitals.[96] This view is strongest among those who perceive themselves to be working class than it is among those who might be considered working class by occupation (C2DEs), suggesting this is an ideological rather than an interest-based position. Politicians who are keen to emphasise competition in public services, or the opposite, resistance to private sector delivery, should be aware that the public remain sceptical about privatisation, but not ideologically wedded to public delivery.

Labour supporters are most likely to have a preference for NHS provision of their care, but more than half (52 per cent) either do not have a preference or would prefer a private or non-profit provider.[97] Conservative supporters are more likely than Labour supporters to prefer private provision (23 per cent as opposed to 13 per cent), while 55 per cent of Liberal Democrats do not have a preference. Voters in the YouGov poll for Policy Exchange tended to agree that choice and competition in public services is 'wasteful and does not actually end up improving services at all' than believe it leads to better standards for all.[98]

Older people in particular are likely to say that the NHS wastes money, with more than 60 per cent of those aged 49 and over agreeing that the NHS often wastes money compared to just over a third of the under-35s, although voters in Scotland are less likely than those in Wales and England to think the NHS often wastes money. Despite the high public attachment to the principles of the NHS, voters are concerned this won't last: nearly half think the NHS will not still be a free universal service in 10 years' time.[99]

> 'I've never got any of my mental issues diagnosed apart from the ADHD as I don't want people to perceive it that if I did get benefits for those things I'm scrounging.' (Voter, Derby)

Policies for health and social care

Every political party likes to portray themselves as the champions of the NHS, hoping some of the favourability of the beloved health service will rub off on them at election time. Yet the reality is that while politicians may proudly cite the courage of post-war politicians in the founding of the universal provision of healthcare, no current politician appears brave enough to reconstitute the NHS for the changing needs of the 21st century and offer anything like the kind of funding the NHS really needs to remain universal. By 2032, the population in England alone is likely to grow to 61 million people, an increase of 8 million from 2012.[100] More than 40 per cent of households are likely to be living alone, with the numbers of people aged over 85 living on their own expected to grow from 573,000 to 1.4 million. The population aged over 65 is growing at a much faster rate than those under 65, rising by 39 per cent over the next 20 years (65-84, and those over 85, by 106 per cent).

Mixed populations are the fastest growing, with differing rates of disease among different groups. This translates into continuing rising demand for health services as the number of older people living with multiple conditions increases, and funding has not kept pace. The challenges for the NHS and social care come not just from the demographics: rising costs, particularly increased prescribing, increase budgetary pressures, and new treatments and technology offer the opportunity for new trials at increased cost. The Office for Budget Responsibility estimates that approximately £30 billion a year more is needed to meet the needs of the ageing and growing population, and no party at the 2017 General Election was willing to commit more than half that in their manifestos.

Arguably the biggest role of government in health is to make sure the NHS has the resources to deal with demand.

The devolved governments in Scotland and Wales have taken different decisions on funding to England, although even then the need exceeds current resources. As costs rise, and the public's recognition of the pressures continues, calls for changes to the NHS funding model will increase. People already have to pay routinely for prescriptions, dental care and optical treatment unless exempted. However, erosion in health universalism such as an insurance-based system would be disastrous for the new working class, whose health prospects already tend to be less favourable than those who are better off. Introducing fees (such as charges for appointments or missed appointments, or for treatments for conditions contributed to by lifestyle) has some public support, but while it may bring in some income and possibly encourage behaviour change, charges for UK residents are likely to push some people in need into debt and worsen their health prospects, turn front-line practitioners into retailers, and seriously undermine the social contract between the state and the citizen.

A popular policy option among the public (including low- and middle-income voters) is to increase charges for foreign nationals coming to the UK using the NHS. Non-residents are meant to be charged for their healthcare, but the UK has a low rate of recouping the costs. In 2015 the UK paid out £674 million to European countries for their health costs but received only £49 million in return, which is partly because Brits run up more bills abroad, but also because the British government is less effective at recovering costs (the figure should be more like £340 million). New rules came into force in October 2017[101] to charge visitors to the UK upfront for the cost of their treatment by any provider that receives NHS funding, which should tackle the issue. Even so, a focus on visitors is not going to produce anything like the sums required to adequately fund the NHS. Political parties also have to bear in mind that over-emphasising the financial contribution from these groups risks sowing social division, therefore any further moves in this direction need to be communicated responsibly.

Funding the NHS isn't, of course, the only challenge. Tackling ever-rising health and care needs requires a shift towards prevention and galvanising people and organisations outside of the NHS to incentivise healthier lifestyles. But no respectable policy agenda aimed at the new working class can dodge the fundamental question of how to meet demand. Policy-makers face a difficult choice. They could continue to pretend marginal spending increases can keep up with patient demand and rising costs, but the reason voter concern about the NHS is rising is because people are already worried about service pressures. They could start to introduce more restrictions on treatments, but there is likely to be a sizeable gap between citizen expectation and provision. They could introduce a health insurance scheme similar to the rest of Europe, but given the strength of the public's attachment to universal provision, this is unlikely to win backing. And all of these options present higher risks to the new working class than the general population.

Policy 1. Introduce citizen service guarantees under a new universal arrangement, such as access to GP appointments within a specified time, limits to waiting times and access to personalised healthcare, funded by a substantial increase in general taxation moving to a specific (hypothecated) NHS tax in time. Without a general tax boost it is likely that universal access will continue to be eroded through charging or even an insurance scheme introduced, which would be a disaster for the new working class. NHS providers can continue to be pragmatic about the delivery of health through private providers. If the public are going to be paying more, then it is also important that local community control and accountability is strengthened so there is a stronger contract between citizen and NHS provision. The National Institute for Health and Care Excellence (NICE) should be given more powers to lower thresholds for determining whether treatments are cost-effective, and increased transparency of decisions taken at a local level about whether non-medically necessary treatments can be offered on the NHS or as a private supplement.

There is little public support for a state-funded social care system, and it has to be recognised that the public believe there are limits to universalism. The health system can be described as in some ways akin to the police, defence or security services in that all members of the public want to know it can be accessed if they or their family need it. The same cannot be said of childcare or social care, as important as they are for those who need them. The basis for a long-term settlement was outlined in the Dilnot report of 2011, which recommended that social care costs should be capped and individuals should pay the first £35,000 of their care if they have more than £100,000 in assets.[102] The Conservatives under Theresa May found out the hard way that public support needed to be built before the electorate are introduced to the implications of using their housing wealth to pay for social care. However, the principles that individuals need to make provision for increased care in older age, but that costs for social care should be capped, were sound.

Policy 2. Introduce a social care insurance scheme administered on behalf of the government via local authorities that can contract out the administration and provision. Like pensions, the emphasis should be on opting out rather than opting in on the basis of contribution rather than working-age people paying for older age, with increasing payments as people age and state-backed guarantees on savings. Local authorities should use behavioural insights to encourage more individuals to opt to defer payment until death, so that their estate is taken into account if they have one.

> 'If you are suffering, how are you meant to hold down a job?' (Voter, Birmingham)

People who are on a low wage or no wages persistently have worse health outcomes than those on higher incomes. Public health and general practitioners know that however effective and well-resourced the health system is, it is only tackling the health components of someone's life, the root cause of which or solution is not always medicine. Somebody may need a prescription. But they might need counselling, or training, or to meet someone who has been in the same situation, or debt advice, or social security. Too often people in need are sent from one service to another, and report how denigrated they feel by the whole experience, rather than a system that is set up to enable people to effect positive changes for themselves with the right support, typically a mix of family, public services, community and friends. Peers can provide encouragement for self-advocacy, to improve the ability of those who can have less of a voice among professionals.

Policy 3. Integrate local health and employment services, addressing the root causes of persistent health problems at a hyper-local level where people are enabled to get the income, training and work support they need as well as get the right interventions with their physical and mental health. Trials are already underway[103] to evaluate the success of integrated approaches, and national government should learn and accelerate interventions that improve earnings and health outcomes. Integrated health and employment services could form the basis of a unified occupation health architecture including the Fit for Work service and Access to Work.[104] Incentivising peer and community support approaches, run by local groups and Clinical Commissioning Groups along with employers and other public services, could enable services to be humanised and centred on the individual. Enabling people to earn credits for community activities like offering skills, trades and support that do not count towards their work allowance hours could allow people to build up confidence and skills. The policy objective needs to be to increase employment, earnings and health outcomes rather than up-front cost savings, and needs to be aligned to a reformed social security system (see Chapter 5).

> 'I'd like to see people on benefits treated with respect. My health has gone downhill since applying for benefits and it has made me lose all confidence, which I'm only getting it back now. A bonus to treating people with respect is a bonus to the NHS as people's health will improve.' (Voter, Glasgow)

Speaking to the values of the new working class

Political parties should be seeking out policies that speak to the values of the new working class and serve as likely triggers to activate their moral foundations. Using the language of their key values is not enough: the rhetoric needs to be backed by symbolic and actual policies that encourage a favourable association between the voter's social identity and the party seeking the vote, deploying the cognitive frame most conducive to conveying the meaning of the policy. Across families, children, education, health and social care are multiple opportunities to tune into the values and moral foundations of the new working class, as well as risks that failure to do so will engender the opposite moral foundation. The dominant values of the new working class are family, fairness, hard work and decency, and the policies set out in this chapter are designed to draw on these values. While any political party would be advised to test out the specifics and the most effective cognitive frames, here are some examples from this chapter.

The *care* moral foundation, which is about being sensitive to need, could be conveyed by a strong universalist policy to guarantee health provision for British citizens. However, proponents also have to trigger *fairness*, which is about the rewards of cooperation without being exploited, and therefore a universalist health system is not just about caring for oneself or others, but also about contribution, a close relationship with the moral foundation of *loyalty*, which is about trust and rewarding team players. Loyalty and *authority* should also be based on contribution rather than on identity, which can risk adverse consequences for others perceived to be outside the given identity, and also triggers the *sanctity* of investing in the health service to bind a group together. The moral foundations can be activated beyond health policies: social care insurance and retaining higher education fees can trigger fairness because they are based on those who benefit most making more of a contribution; and symbolic policies to preserve family time and children's prospects can activate the sanctity of a shared investment for the future. *Liberty*, which resists attempted domination, could be summed up in a more assertive approach to the use of public services where individuals are more in control. Any policies involving the home must be treated with particular caution: while it might be considered fair to account for the cost of the home in someone's estate to set against their social care bill when they die, the home negatively activates both sanctity and liberty. It does not mean the policy cannot be pursued, but it needs a long-run approach to gauge the successful means of framing the policy.

The great examples of making policies symbolic and memorable are usually unified by the way they make the pledge about families and individuals rather than a more abstract policy goal, for example, a guaranteed GP appointment within a certain time, or class size limit of 30 pupils, or the right to own a council home. They also have to be credible: there have been a number of imitators of the right to home ownership since Margaret Thatcher's policy, but none have had the demonstrable delivery that she did, which can undermine trust among the electorate. Far from policies not mattering, voters actually do remember policies, but overdoing rhetoric on families or the right to buy, for example, can lead to fatigue unless it is accompanied by memorable action. Families, education and health provide multiple opportunities to speak to the interests of the new working class, if backed by meaningful symbols likely to make a difference to their core concerns. Families and individuals are, of course, shaped by wider society, and it is to the modern economy, work and welfare, where it could be said that the origins of the new working class are, to which we now turn.

5

The economy, work and welfare

'When I hear the word "economy" I think of corrupt politicians playing the economy for personal and professional gain.' (Voter, Port Talbot)

It has been received wisdom since the Bill Clinton campaign famously used the phrase, 'It's the economy, stupid' during his successful bid for the US presidency in 1992 that the performance of the economy is the single biggest determinant of an election outcome. Even though the vote for the UK to leave the EU illustrated that voters consider societal factors as important as economic ones, how the performance of the economy translates into people's individual circumstances really matters to winning votes. Successive chancellors have introduced voter-friendly tax or spend measures in the run-up to a general election, observing that there is a direct relationship between how well the economy performs in the months before a general election, and whether people vote for the incumbents.[1] Analysis of the 2017 General Election showed that those who thought their household finances had got worse were much more likely to vote for the opposition than the incumbent Conservative government.[2] To policy specialists, the economy, work and incomes are different things. To an individual, they mean their prospects of earning, what they and their family can afford to buy and their living conditions, the extent to which they have a choice over their circumstances, and their quality of life. Work and the economy set the context in which non-material factors are played out.

The main reason social class distinctions have become so blurred is because work has changed so dramatically since there was a more cemented view of class, closely associated with occupation. Over the past 40 years, work in Britain has undergone a revolution. Technology, industry, educational levels, trade union representation, women's participation in the labour market and combining work with home life have fundamentally altered the nature of work, and with it, the nature of social class in modern Britain. For the new working class, work tends to be non-graduate and less well paid, more difficult to progress in, and a proportion will either not be working due to health or caring responsibilities, or will be moving in and out of work. More say they struggle to make ends meet or 'just about manage' on their income than those who are better off, and have to cope with fluctuations in their incomes. Personal finances are the second front of mind concern whether or not people are living on a low income,[3] and for those who are, money or debt is their biggest worry.[4] People on low incomes will routinely report having to budget very tightly to afford essentials like food and heating, and having to make difficult choices about priorities. Incomes have flat-lined for the new working class in the past decade-and-a-half: according to the Resolution Foundation's barometer on living standards, typical real incomes after housing costs among low- to middle-income households were lower in 2016-17 than in 2003-04.[5]

Material experiences of the economy, work and welfare are highly dependent on geography. There is a lot of low pay within our big cities; for example, 58 per cent of men working part time in the capital earn less than the voluntary London Living Wage.[6] There is a significant gap in pay between London and the South East and the rest of the UK. The average weekly pay of workers in Blackpool, at £333, is half that of those in Southwark, at £639.[7] Areas of low pay also tend to be areas of lower levels of educational attainment, lower social mobility and fewer professional occupations. Graduates in those areas tend to leave in search of employment elsewhere, and this can be a countrywide problem, not just regional variance: 30 per cent of Welsh-domiciled graduates were employed in England six months after graduation.[8]

Overall employment has remained high during a period of economic turbulence, and the National Minimum Wage has effectively abolished extreme poverty pay. But due to the UK's endemic low pay problem, getting a job does not guarantee that your family will not be living in poverty. And the likelihood of someone struggling to make ends meet will be greater depending

Figure 10: Wage map of Britain

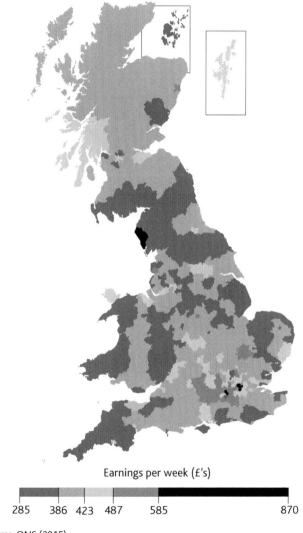

Earnings per week (£'s)

285   386   423   487   585   870

Source: ONS (2015)

on where they live, their ethnicity, having a disability or needing to care for someone who does, and their education and skills. The benefits of the UK's prosperous economy are deeply uneven, and there is no clear route map to address this inequality overall or its worst excesses at the bottom end.

The economy

For many people, the economy is understood in relation to their household circumstances. Low- to middle-income households spend a much greater proportion of their budget on essentials like heating and food than higher-income households, so changes in prices have a particularly big impact on the money they have available. Between 2008 and 2014, the cost of essentials went up three times faster than average earnings and twice as fast as inflation, and lower-income households experienced higher inflation.[9] People with a disability or health condition generally face even higher costs, which is partially compensated for by the benefits system, but even so, it is reported that 69 per cent of disabled people struggle with or fall behind on bills.[10] Households on low to middle incomes are also less likely to have financial security now and in the long term: around half of those on middle incomes have savings of over £1,500 compared to a third of those on the lowest incomes, whereas the vast majority of mid- to high-income households have financial security in the form of savings worth more than £1,500.[11]

> 'I may not have food at home at some points as prices have gone up so much, I feel like I'm living on the poverty line sometimes.' (Voter, Oldham)

Work and gaining an income is a means to an end for many people, and while voters report wanting enough to have security with a bit left over to spend, they do not constantly aspire to be rich, or even envy the rich. A YouGov poll of voters showed that nearly two-thirds of people from all social classes agree that they are 'generally happy with what I have in life; as long as I have my health, friends and family I do not aspire to having more.' Around a quarter demonstrated a desire for greater material gain: 'I am keen to move up in life, to get a bigger home, higher income and more luxuries in life', and this was less strongly felt by occupational social classes C2, D and E[12] (manual workers and those on low incomes; see the endnote for a detailed explanation of occupational social grades[13]). Concern about the levels of poverty and inequality has been rising over the past few years;[14] however, it is not clear whether the concern is about the very poorest or richest, or both. Inequality and the behaviour of the very richest does not present as a front of mind concern for the new working class, and while reducing inequality was added as a concern to the Scottish Social Attitudes survey in 2015 by the Scottish Government, only 4 per cent of respondents said it was their priority.[15] However, their own family's material circumstances are of central importance.

> '"Economy" means bills and economising on heating: personal economy. It's difficult when you're not earning much or receiving enough. In this country people do not make enough to have a reasonable standard of living.' (Voter, Port Talbot)

Public attitudes to the economy

Public policy on the economy over the past few years has been characterised by a drive towards reducing the national deficit delivered in part by constraining public spending. There have been more recent signs that the public is wearying of austerity; however, public attitudes' data shows that cuts in government spending have never enjoyed majority support. At present, less than a third of the public support cuts to help the economy, compared to 43 per cent in 1996.[16] Nearly half of the public now say that the government should increase taxes and spend more, a higher proportion than at any time in the last 10 years, while an only slightly smaller proportion think taxes and spending should stay the same as they are now.[17] This pattern is fairly similar across all income groups. However, a majority also say that those on low incomes are taxed too much,[18] even though some on low incomes do not pay Income Tax or National

Insurance, just VAT. Around a third say taxes are too high for people on middle incomes, and a quarter say they are too high for those on high incomes. Views on tax and spend are likely to be highly susceptible to medium-term political and economic conditions, yet even so, it is interesting to note that the public is roughly divided between those who say tax and spend more and those who say keep it as it is, with a small minority of about 5-10 per cent who say tax and spend less.

It is likely that that the public is not particularly ideological about the economy. A poll of voters found nearly half agreed with the statement 'Government can be a force for good, and it should do more to offer ordinary working people help and assistance at every stage of their life', whereas a third chose 'Government should be as small as possible, it should provide a safety net when people are in real trouble, but the rest of the time it should leave ordinary working people to get on with their lives.'[19]

If there were to be increased public spending, people's top priorities would be the same as they have always been: health and education.[20] There is some, but not majority, support for redistributing income from the better-off to the less well-off, and there is not much more support for this among the lowest

Figure 11: Support for redistribution, according to income

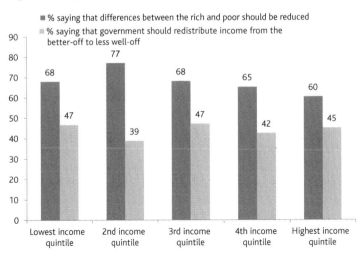

Source: Taylor et al (2017, Figure 4.2)

incomes (47 per cent) than the highest (45 per cent).[21] While this has risen since the financial crisis, it is not a strong endorsement for highly redistributive policies, even among the new working class, and support for redistribution is lowest among the second income quintile (39 per cent). Having said that, there is clearly an awareness of inequality between groups, as majorities across all categories support reducing differences between the rich and the less well-off (and support for this is highest among the second income quintile). The new working class would support higher taxes on the middle- to better-off sections of society if it is to pay for increased spending on health and education; they want to see inequalities between rich and poor tackled but do not support heavy redistribution of income.

The public is generally quite sceptical about the motivations of big business. Overall three-quarters of the public agree that 'The people who run big companies tend to be more concerned with their own pay and bonuses than with treating their staff well and providing a good service to their customers', and people who perceive themselves to be working class (subjective class status) tend to be even stronger in their view.[22] Overwhelmingly, people think that those who are well off and who run big business benefit from the way the economy works, and this does not differ by social class.[23] Over 60 per cent of the public believe tax avoidance is unacceptable.[24]

Recent analysis of the British public after the vote to leave the EU reveals that many perceive price rises by businesses after the vote as opportunistic.[25] However, there are limits to the extent to which the public believe million-pound plus salaries can be curtailed, and even among social class C2DEs, only 40 per cent support a change in the law to ban them.[26] In general, there is less support for reducing regulation of business than there used to be before the financial crisis, and there is strong support for an active government to support industry. Eighty-three per cent agree that it should be the government's responsibility to provide industry with the help it needs to grow, and to develop new products and technology. About the same high proportion think it should be the government's responsibility to keep prices under control, and the same proportion think the government should finance projects to create new jobs. There is less support

Figure 12: Public attitudes to the government's role in the economy

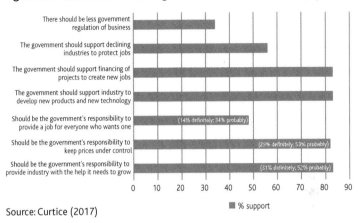

than there was 10 years ago for government to support declining industries to protect jobs, but it is still relatively strong, with 56 per cent in favour and only 14 per cent against.[27] Financial policies that the government could introduce that were rated most popular by voters in occupational classes C2, D and E were freezing energy bills, raising the personal tax allowance (which takes low earners out of tax, but gives a bigger benefit to higher earners), reducing VAT, reducing taxes on petrol and abolishing or reducing the licence fee.[28]

Policies for the economy

Attitudinal data reveals that the public is not particularly ideological when it comes to the economy, even though approaches to the economy tend to be a symbolic indicator of political leaning. For example, redistribution is more heavily associated with the left of centre, and lower taxes and reduced spending with the right. But what matters most to the new working class is what makes a difference to their incomes, their prospects and their financial security, and they are less wedded to the means of delivery. The challenge for political parties seeking election is how to demonstrate that they have the right policies and tone to create an environment where business can prosper and create jobs, at the same time not appearing as though they are more aligned to big business than the interests of the new working-class voter.

British politics now seems to be transitioning out of a phase of hegemony of laissez-faire economics into something much less certain and likely to be dominated in the short term by the parameters established by the terms under which Britain exits the EU. Theresa May began to signal this shift with a more interventionist agenda, reflecting widespread concern that the state in retreat leaves citizens ill protected from the vagaries of globalisation. The British public recognises that there is no going back to a pre-digital, pre-deindustrialisation era, but are not convinced by politicians sitting back while companies en masse pass costs on to consumers without consequence or evade their tax obligations. It is not surprising that after one of the most severe global financial crises in history that the public wants an assertive and effective role for government in the modern economy. However, public appetite for income redistribution is limited.

There is a significant disparity between economic opportunities in London and the South East and the rest of the UK, despite the fact that three-quarters of the British population do not live there. London and the South East account for a third of the UK's economy, and have 24 times as much spent on their infrastructure than the North East.[29] While many places are thriving, in particular the big cities, prosperity and opportunity are unevenly experienced within places as well as between them. Attempts to increase private and state investment into the rest of the UK are not bringing about the transformative change that is required to rebalance the British economy, and while the election of a new era of city and regional mayors brings a welcome political focus, without backing in the form of infrastructure and investment, the mayors will be curtailed in their ability to build local economies that work for all. There is significant political gain for the party that can convince the new working class in constituencies all across the UK that their employment and earnings potential will be best served by a party that can lead national efforts to drive inward investment into the regions of the UK. The creation of the 'Northern Powerhouse' by former Chancellor George Osborne was recognition by the Conservatives that their electoral prospects were linked to the North of England's long-term prosperity, but without real policies and buy-in across his party, it may have been established too late in his chancellorship to make the difference it needs.

Policy 1. Drive a new era of regional economic growth that puts positive improvements for citizens at its heart, and industrial strategy organised around the goal of good work. Provide access to high-quality jobs for people from the locality, particularly those who form the bulk of the new working class, with a much more ambitious approach to skills. Moves to create good work should be backed by financial incentives, such as tax breaks for firms that provide decent quality jobs for people at risk of financial hardship. Political and economic power is highly concentrated in London, and regional investment should be aligned to greater political devolution and accountability. High-speed transport connections are vital. At its core, parties seeking success need an active, long-term industrial strategy that supports industries likely to provide inclusive growth in regions of the UK that most need it, backed by financial incentives and a positive climate for business that fulfils its social obligations through supporting the skills and educational development of the local population.

Government – locally and nationally – can play an important role with the significant purchasing power its £45 billion expenditure on goods and services in the UK economy brings.[30] Leaving the EU should be an opportunity to establish how the UK's public purchasing could be used more actively to support UK firms. Clearly government will not want to apply this too crudely, as signs of economic nationalism ordinarily entail a retaliatory response from overseas governments. However, for many citizens, it is common sense that the UK government should be able to support UK businesses if they are also achieving value for money for taxpayers. This could be through contracts to UK businesses, in particular, small- to medium-sized enterprises operating in areas of the UK that need a jobs boost, or it could also mean greater obligations on contractors bidding for public spending to ensure they meet local social responsibilities such as participating in employer-backed colleges to increase skills acquisitions for locals. While the feasibility of this depends on the outcome and application of the terms under which the UK leaves the EU, it represents an opportunity to put social impact at the core of British business.

Policy 2. Boost UK business through government spending. Introduce new rules to allow UK businesses to be selected for government contracts if they can demonstrate they are creating good quality jobs locally and participating in the local economy such as by providing employer input into local colleges. Buying locally can make a big difference to the local economy. More local wealth has been generated and retained in Preston following a voluntary initiative to buy local: an extra £75 million a year is being spent within the city, and the top 300 suppliers have created an extra 800 jobs in 2016 alone.[31] Local and city political leadership can make a significant difference, especially if UK businesses who take up the call are backed with incentives.

Consumer faith in the fair operation of markets has taken a significant battering over the last few years. The financial crisis that began in the depths of the sub-prime mortgage market in Florida in 2007, and entailed the government's emergency rescue of the UK's banking sector, revealed the inadequacy of the regulatory regime that may have alerted government earlier to or prevented the crisis. The Libor scandal, where banks colluded to hide their true interest rates to increase their profits, compounded the view that markets were operating to the benefit of the very rich.

Seemingly never-ending price rises for energy, when companies always seem to pass on an increase in costs to the consumer but never a decrease, mean that consumers can feel like they are getting a raw deal. While this is the case for people at any income level, this is a particular issue for the new working class who spend a greater proportion of their incomes on essentials, and low-income consumers are less likely to change providers than mid- to higher-income consumers. Politicians have looked powerless or collusive in response: failing to extract fair taxes from global corporates like Google and Amazon, or offering public denunciations without policy change. Former Labour leader Ed Miliband showed that there was a political dividend in standing up to disregard for the consumer with the announcement of an energy price freeze if Labour came to power (which they didn't), and Theresa May included a partial energy tariff cap in the 2017 Conservative manifesto.[32] Both were attempts to relate to consumer disenchantment with the behaviour of corporates, without having a comprehensive or robust approach to making modern markets work.

Policy 3. Establish a consumer-champion programme to modernise the state's approach to market competition. A symbolic policy such as an energy price cap would be an appealing policy for the new working class, but the reforms would have to go deeper to effect change and prove to the public that the party was serious – for example, extending the remit and powers of the sector regulators to protect consumers from excessive price rises on essential goods and services; giving the Inland Revenue stronger leadership on enforcing tax payments for global corporates; giving tax breaks to firms that adopt social responsibilities to reward responsible business behaviour; and making social obligations a condition of government contracts.

Work

Picturing a 'typical' working-class person in Britain 30 or 40 years ago would probably would have brought to mind a worker employed in a large workplace like a factory, doing partly-skilled manual work, most likely a man, and most likely White. That has all changed. Just about every aspect of the way we work is different. The new working class undertake hundreds of different types of jobs in today's economy, employed as cleaners, shop workers, bar tenders, cooks, carers, teaching assistants, secretaries, delivery workers, and so on. They may have a formal full-time contract but are more likely than middle-class workers to work part time with different hours and shifts, sometimes by choice, sometimes not. More recently, they are more likely to be self-employed and not have a formal employer at all. Or the place they work in every day may be different to the firm that employs them because they are contractors. There is also a reasonable proportion who combine work with caring and other responsibilities, or who don't work at all. As Chapter 2 stated in defining the new working class, if there ever was a 'typical' working-class person, there certainly isn't now.

The vast majority of the new working class will be in work. However, almost as many of those who are in work in the lowest income group are not in work because they are in education, experiencing ill health, caring for someone or looking after the home. Just 14 per cent of this category are unemployed, and could be assumed to be able to work.[33] While a higher proportion of the second bottom income group are working (58 per cent compared to 38 per cent of the lowest income category), nearly one in five are also not working due to being in education, caring, ill or looking after the home.

Figure 13: Working status, according to income

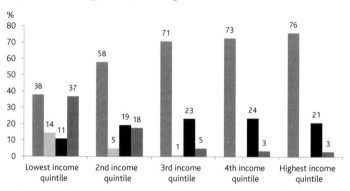

Source: Taylor et al (2017, Figure 2.3)

The work profile of those in the middle-income category is similar to that in middle- to higher-income groups, with over 70 per cent working in each. As might be expected, most people in the new working class are employed, and there is a strong association with work and income. The data highlights two interesting issues to note that are relevant to work and welfare. Comparatively few people who are not working are classed as unemployed, and there is a much bigger proportion of those on low incomes who do not work because of ill health, disability, caring responsibilities, or because they are in education or looking after the home (retired people are represented separately). The second issue it shows is that most adults on low to mid incomes are in work. This is not a new finding.

The Joseph Rowntree Foundation, among others, has tracked this for several years, and reports that over half of those in poverty live in a household where someone is working.[34] But the reality for politicians is that while they continue to repeat the mantra that the best route out of poverty is work, this remains a political aspiration and not an economic reality for the millions of people trapped on low pay. Low pay is not in and of itself necessarily a problem, as for lots of people it will be temporary, and many on low pay will be living in a household with a higher earner. The main issue with the UK's low pay problem is that too many people are stuck there. Three-quarters of low-paid employees are still in low pay a decade later.[35] There is a specific and problematic link to disability, gender and ethnicity, in that non-White workers, women and people with disabilities are all disadvantaged in the labour market compared to White, male, non-disabled people, and over-represented in the new working class. The new working class is multi-ethnic, of all abilities, and more likely to be female than male.

> 'I voted Brexit because I thought it should make wages rises because employers will have to pay a decent wage rather than exploiting immigrants as cheap labour.' (Voter, Scarborough)

Public attitudes to work

Work or finding a job is of more concern to people who comprise the new working class than it is to those who are better off, with a quarter of those on the lowest incomes saying work or finding a job is an important issue for them.[36] Most people felt able to do something to improve their problems about work or find a job.[37]

There is an increase in perceived job quality and satisfaction among all groups, including the new working class. More people say they have what counts as a 'good job' these days, involving characteristics such as the work being interesting and having good opportunities for advancement.[38] Sixty-two per cent of those who are occupationally working class say their job has four or more positive attributes compared to 42 per cent in 1989 (this compares to an increase from 72 to 77 per cent for the highest social class). Overall the proportion of workers in the economy with a 'good job' has increased, and the gap between the social classes of those with a 'good job' has reduced. However, those on lower incomes are significantly less satisfied with their jobs than those on higher incomes[39] and those in routine or semi-routine occupations were much more likely than those in professional or managerial occupations to say that a job is solely about the money earned.[40]

Figure 14: Jobs in modern Britain

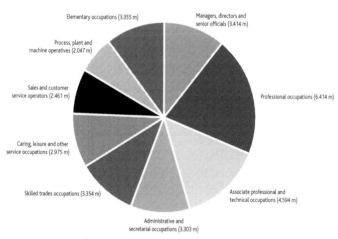

Elementary occupations (3.355 m)

Managers, directors and senior officials (3.414 m)

Process, plant and machine operatives (2.047 m)

Sales and customer service operators (2.461 m)

Professional occupations (6.414 m)

Caring, leisure and other service occupations (2.975 m)

Skilled trades occupations (3.354 m)

Associate professional and technical occupations (4.594 m)

Administrative and secretarial occupations (3.303 m)

Source: ONS (2017)

Across the whole public, there is a gap between the job attributes people say are important, and what they perceive they have from their job.[41] For example, 93 per cent say job security is important, yet only 65 per cent say they have this; 66 per cent say high income is important, but only 26 per cent say they have this; 81 per cent say good opportunities for advancement are important, but only 34 per cent say they have this. It is a reasonable assumption that this gap between expectation and reality will be even higher among the new working class.

> 'If we were actually paid when we were off sick that would be such a huge weight off my shoulders. I panic if I can tell I've got even a cold coming on because I cannot afford not to work.' (Voter, Eastleigh)

Although work appears to offer more positive attributes to the new working class today than it used to, there has been a significant drop in perceived job security in a relatively short space of time. In 2005, 71 per cent of people in semi-routine and routine jobs said they had job security, which fell to 60 per cent in 2015.[42] Job security has increased since 2005 for professional and managerial workers (65 per cent in 2005 to 67 per cent in 2015); however, given that the public debate about job security has focused mainly on the lower end of the labour market, it is interesting to note that there is not that much difference between professional and managerial workers who say they have job security, and routine and semi-routine workers.

There is, however, a more marked disparity between occupations in those who have a say in how their daily work is organised. Fifty-seven per cent of people in routine and semi-routine occupations now say they are not free to decide how their daily work is organised compared to 42 per cent in 2005.[43] Yet there has been an increase from 28 per cent in 2005 to 39 per cent in 2015 of those in professional and managerial occupations who say they are free to decide how their daily work is organised. This could be an indication that the benefits of technological and cultural change at work are being played out unevenly across occupational classes.

All social classes are more stressed at work than they were, with professional and managerial workers and those aged 35-44 most likely to feel stressed. However, those in semi-routine and routine jobs saw the greatest increase in constant stress between 2005 (1 per cent) and 2015 (10 per cent).[44]

The public's expectations of the role of government in relation to employment are changing gradually over time. Over the past 30 years there has been a fall in the proportion of people

Figure 15: What people experienced in work, 2005-15

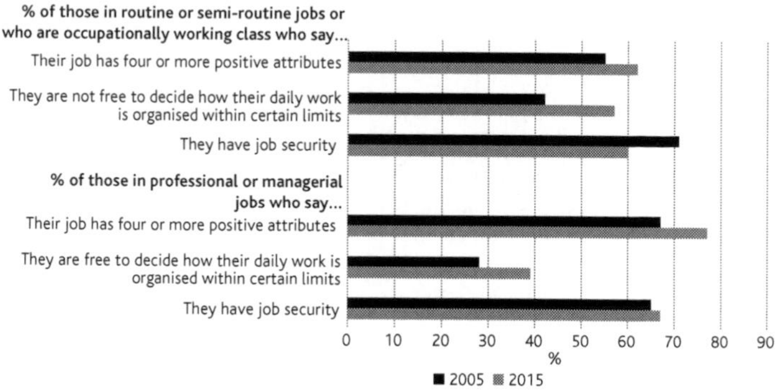

Source: McKay and Simpson (2016)

who say that government should provide a job for everyone who wants one, from 65 per cent in 1996 to 48 per cent in 2016.[45] More people on low to middle incomes than those on higher incomes say it is the government's responsibility to provide a job for everyone who wants one, but even so, this has declined and is far less than the proportion who think it is the government's responsibility to provide healthcare for the sick, for example. Likewise, 56 per cent of the public think it should be the government's responsibility to provide a decent standard of living for the unemployed.[46]

Although these proportions have fallen over time, they could also be reflective of the relatively high employment rates enjoyed in the UK since unemployment peaked in the mid-1980s at more than 3 million and reached nearly that level in the early 1990s. Most people agree that most people who are unemployed could find a job if they tried hard enough,[47] and just 16 per cent support more government spending on unemployment benefits.[48] Overall, expectations of government have not declined much in other areas of public policy in the past 20 years, such as providing housing, keeping prices under control and providing industry with the help it needs to grow,[49] suggesting that responses are shaped by the view that people can get a job if they want one, rather than any overall view that the state should retreat.

Policies for work

High employment and abolishing extreme poverty pay are significant achievements of the last 20 years. The issues the new working class face in relation to work are serious, however: long-term low pay that leaves them unable to save for the future, insecurity, a lack of opportunity to progress, and much of their prospects in the labour market related to geographical location or individual characteristics of being female, from a non-White minority ethnic group, with caring responsibilities, or with a disability or health condition. And this is before the full effects of automation impact on jobs at all levels, in industries from retail to hospitality.

Theoretically there is a chance that the supply of low-wage labour is set to fall due to a dip in immigration, thereby increasing the price of currently cheap labour, but even if this were to occur, it could result in the loss of low-wage jobs without the prospects of an alternative. In addition, it would go against the last 40 years' form for an economic gear change to benefit the least well-off. One of the major risks for the new working class is not just their vulnerability to automation, but how ill equipped they are compared to higher skilled workers to adapt or change jobs. Of course, automation is not just the only driver of industrial change: companies failing, re-locating or re-structuring happens all the time. But one of the characteristics that members of the new working class share is their likelihood of not holding a university degree, and it is the increased skills and qualifications that come with higher education that equip many workers to change jobs or careers, and therefore so disadvantages non-graduates. Too many people in the new working class are trapped by receiving an education that did not equip them well enough in the first place into jobs that do not pay enough to make ends meet, and are stuck there due to lack of opportunity and skills to move on.

From the perspective of the new working class, the priorities for policies about work are ones that promote jobs with security, a decent wage, the opportunity to advance, and that are interesting. Employers in the private and public sectors are primarily responsible for those things, but government has an important role to play where the labour market does not fulfil citizens' expectations. At the same time, government needs to not be so interventionist in its directions that it creates a negative environment for job creation, and ends up deterring companies, whether home-grown or from overseas, from investing in jobs in Britain. Job security is fast emerging as the big priority for working people, and a party that can demonstrate it is committed to improving security in the modern economy is likely to be closely listened to by voters.

> 'Getting paid for travel time doesn't feel like a bonus or a perk from our employer, it feels like a basic human right. But nine times out of ten in care it doesn't happen. So that's definitely the one I'd pick.'
> (Voter, Grimsby)

Policy 1. Create an employment rights floor to safeguard all workers from practices that unfairly decrease their job security, such as guaranteeing sick pay regardless of employment status and stamping out non-payment of waiting time. Flexible working practices can benefit both worker and employer, but over time it has become too easy for employers to evade basic employment rights, creating insecurity for the individual and unfair competition with better employers. Employers should be incentivised to adopt working practices that create security, not rewarded for a race to the bottom on employment conditions. While the focus for public debate has been on the increased use of zero-hours contracts that do not provide a guarantee of hours, blanket bans or guaranteed hours after a fixed period are likely to create unforeseen consequences (like workers being discharged just before the flexible period). A package on security at work would be better placed being targeted at clamping down on extreme practices such as routinely giving workers daily notice for work that has been practised in the US, before they take hold in the UK. A charter on day one of a worker's employment rights, whether contracted or directly, was one suggestion by the Taylor review of modern working practices[50] that could underpin a new job security package.

As well as the new working class being much less likely to have a university degree, workers who missed going to university first time around are also less likely to have had access to training, further education or skills development.[51] The recent Taylor review highlighted the problem: over half of those in the lowest socioeconomic category have not participated in any training since they left education. Given the pace of technological and global change, as well as the rising working age as people live longer, many middle-aged workers are being left further and further behind.

> 'Companies used to have a responsibility to train and educate a local workforce. That isn't the case these days because they can go abroad to find the skills.'
> (Voter, Clacton-on-Sea)

Policy 2. Inspire a learning revolution for adult workers, in adult education and at work, with a new alliance between employers and government. Meet all basic skills needs including digital skills by 2030.[52] Establish a high-level quality standard for apprenticeships, an employer-run institute,[53] better routes into higher skilled tech apprenticeships and ban low-quality apprenticeships. Introduce a second chance career fund to help older workers retrain.[54] Costs for training for low-paid workers in sectors such as social care should be written off, especially in Scotland, which is still paying higher education fees for middle-class students.

One of the unforeseen consequences of the opening up of access to higher education, at the same time as the proportion of semi-skilled jobs declined, has been the decrease in status of non-graduate professions. Professions that used to be considered part of the working class, like nursing, have become graduate occupations. While those moves have increased the standing of many professions as well as the standards they work to, social, cultural and economic disparities have been created between those who hold a degree and those who don't. Of course it is possible to have a university degree and still be, or perceive yourself to be, working class, but a university degree is generally a signifier of upward mobility, and the fact that many young people are going to higher education should not mean that those who don't face such a dismal pool of options and prospects for decent living standards in adulthood. Higher education is in need of reform, as argued in Chapter 4, but that aside, the status of non-graduate occupations needs to be improved so that it gives people respect and dignity at work, whatever their level of attainment. Within this, the lack of availability of good quality part-time jobs reinforces the pay differential between groups, in particular for people with disabilities and those with health conditions, and those who have caring responsibilities. The relative disadvantage by non-White minority ethnic groups, women and people with disabilities needs to be tackled, and by focusing on improving prospects and progression into higher paid jobs by sector and profession as well as by characteristic, efforts are more likely to have a tangible impact.

Policy 3. Government should lead the way on a campaign for good work, with a particular focus on non-graduate and part-time jobs. While employers will lead good practice, politicians can provide strategic national and local leadership towards employment that provides opportunity, security, training, employee benefits, flexibility and progression. 'Good Work' standard could be developed with support from government, employers in the private, public and voluntary sectors, and with the trade unions. Government can ensure the technological infrastructure is in place to enable flexible, part-time working as well as practically incentivising employers through the tax system. Priority sectors should be retail, care and hospitality, which is where low-paid jobs are concentrated. Clear targets should be set for decreasing the gap in employment for particular minority ethnic groups and those who are disabled, and employment support devolved so employers can work locally to strengthen opportunities. Many people with disabilities can and want to work, but struggle to find employers willing to offer them the kind of flexible working that will work with their conditions. Increasing the availability of good-quality part-time and flexible jobs could bring many people with disabilities and those with caring responsibilities into employment.

Welfare

How people feel about welfare can be more of a signifier of their ideological leaning than other topics. It evokes more ideologically based responses, where party affiliation and attitudes to tax and spend, and redistribution, play a role. Probably more than any other topic, welfare illustrates how the moral foundations can be triggered, both deliberately and inadvertently, by policy and rhetoric. Care and fairness in particular, and their opposite notions of harm and cheating, are often called on by politicians to justify policy on welfare. When former Chancellor George Osborne announced that he was going to make £10 billion worth of cuts in welfare, mainly to working-age adults and their children, he set out to activate the moral foundation of cheating among listeners of Radio 4's 'Today' programme when he said, '... our conception of fairness, and this is perhaps where we differ from the Labour party, also extends to the welfare system. We also think it's unfair that when that person leaves their home early in the morning, they pull the door behind them, they're going off to do their job, they're looking at their next-door neighbour, the blinds are down, and that family is living a life on benefits. That is unfair as well, and we are going to tackle that as part of tackling this country's economic problems.'[55]

Demonstrating an awareness that the Labour Party could have been perceived by voters to be too lenient towards benefit recipients in the past, Labour's Shadow Work and Pensions Secretary Rachel Reeves said, in an interview with *The Guardian* newspaper, 'We are not the party of people on benefits. We don't want to be seen, and we're not, the party to represent those who are out of work. Labour are a party of working people, formed for and by working people.'[56] Where a party stands on welfare has a disproportionate effect on how it is perceived by the electorate compared to other topics, therefore placing the policy and the rhetoric effectively on welfare matters to winning voters over.

Welfare has been a focus of public policy over the last few years, simultaneously the target for public spending cuts and the subject of a major overhaul of the benefits system. At times, those two policy objectives have sat at odds with one another. Despite the implied distinction between benefit recipients and those in work, most of those of working age who are in receipt of social security spending (welfare benefits) are in work. A system that was born as a form of collective social insurance against unemployment now has to grapple with a growing population that is living longer, more people with disabilities and fluctuating conditions, low pay that is not enough on its own to meet minimum needs, and soaring costs of housing.

The labour market is more flexible and less secure than it once was, and a million people lose work every three months while another million find work. Over a lifetime, most people will be a recipient of welfare in one form or another.[57] As John Hills points out in his book on the welfare state, 'There is no them and us – just us.' By defining themselves as for the in-work not the out-of-work (or in Osborne's case, one can assume he means the out-of-work and asleep), politicians are making a pitch to voters but storing up a policy muddle for themselves. And the thorniest issue of all is that the public is least supportive of curtailing benefits to pensioners, even though the largest area of social security spending is on the state pension which enjoys a 'triple lock' to ensure it is uprated with inflation and costs while other benefits for working-age adults have been frozen

Figure 16: Social security spending in 2016

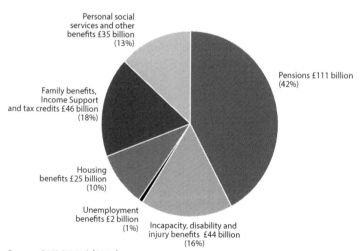

Personal social services and other benefits £35 billion (13%)

Pensions £111 billion (42%)

Family benefits, Income Support and tax credits £46 billion (18%)

Housing benefits £25 billion (10%)

Unemployment benefits £2 billion (1%)

Incapacity, disability and injury benefits £44 billion (16%)

Source: ONS Digital (2016)

since 2012. So what do the new working class want from the social security system, and how can welfare policies be formed to appeal to their views?

Public attitudes to welfare

Across the public as a whole, there is relatively high support for the welfare state, although public attitudes to welfare spending have hardened over the last few decades,[58] most markedly among Labour Party supporters.[59] There is strong support for the cap on welfare benefits to not exceed what people can earn in work, as well as low trust in the effectiveness of the benefits system overall.[60] There is some support for reducing welfare spending on the unemployed and couples without children;[61] however, there appears to have been a softening in the response to welfare reform over the past few years. Fifty per cent say 'cutting welfare benefits would damage too many people's lives', with only 16 per cent disagreeing, and those on the lowest incomes are only slightly more likely to agree with this than those on the highest.[62] This may be a result of the high-profile effects of welfare cuts, such as delays in benefit receipt, increased use of financial sanctions to penalise those who are deemed not to comply, and the rise in use of local foodbanks (by working adults in particular).

NatCen found that views on welfare tended to be driven by ideology (party affiliation, attitude to redistribution, attitudes to tax and spend), and measures of self-interest (age, income, whether or not they were benefit recipients) also have a role to play.[63] They found that supporting the Conservatives, having A-levels or GCSEs and being retired were all associated with thinking that benefits for unemployed people were too high.[64] A majority of people on low to middle incomes think it should be the government's responsibility to provide a decent standard of living for the unemployed, but this is not shared by those on higher incomes (65 per cent of lowest incomes and 67 per cent second income quintile, compared to 47 per cent of the top two income groups). Every income group thinks that it should be the government's responsibility to provide a decent standard of living for the old.[65]

'When you go down it seems their main concern is to get you to quit welfare, not even about getting a job. If there's no job then you always worry you are about to get sanctioned because they say you haven't tried hard enough. If you're sanctioned it's scary because you'll have to go to the foodbank.' (Voter, Glasgow)

Support for welfare varies according to the group the benefit is intended for, as well as who is answering the question. Seventy-five per cent of the public think more should be spent on people who care for those who are sick or have a disability, 61 per cent support more spending on parents who work on very low incomes and people with disabilities who cannot work, 49 per cent say retired people, 36 per cent say single parents, and 17 per cent say unemployed people.[66] Those on middle to higher incomes are more likely to think the level of benefits for unemployed people is too low than those on lower to middle incomes.[67]

Most people (60 per cent) say that unemployment benefit should be received for a limited time, and four in five say those on unemployment benefits should be required to take a job even if it pays the minimum wage, is a short-term contract or they are not interested in it.[68] People appear to be more sympathetic to those with children than the unemployed, with a majority agreeing that the government should top up wages for working couples with children and for lone parents.[69] Most people think that those without children should look after themselves rather than the government topping up their wages.

The public feels very strongly about benefit fraud, and vastly over-estimates the level of benefit fraud that actually takes place. Ninety-one per cent think using false information to support a claim is usually wrong, and estimate that on average 34 out of 100 claimants has done this, when the government's estimate is that 0.3–4.1 per cent of benefit spending is fraudulent.[70] The proportion of people who think that benefit claimants are 'fiddling' is at its lowest level since 1986, but people are tougher on benefit fraud than tax evasion.[71] While only a fifth think that 'many people who get social security don't really deserve any help', the remaining proportions are evenly split between those

Figure 17: Percentage believing people who get social security 'don't really deserve any help', according to income

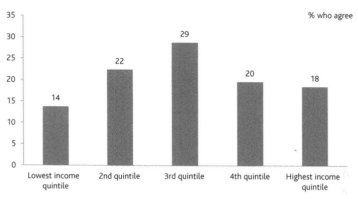

Source: Taylor et al (2017, Figure 5.2)

who disagreed and those who picked neither option, suggesting there is significant ambiguity among the public about the fairness of the current benefits system.

Those on lowest to middle incomes (lowest and second quintile) are much more likely than other groups (43 per cent compared to 26-30 per cent) to agree that the reason some people on benefits cheat the system is that they don't get enough to live on, and are slightly more likely than other groups to agree (30 per cent compared to 21-23 per cent) that a lot of false benefit claims are the result of confusion rather than dishonesty.[72] People who are occupationally working class but see themselves as middle class tend to be tougher on benefits, for example, a higher proportion disagree that stories about benefits fraud are overblown.[73] All groups felt it was more important for the government to stop people claiming benefits to which they are not entitled (55 per cent) than to help people claim benefits to which they are entitled (32 per cent).[74] People on lower incomes tend to have stricter views on EU migrants' access to benefits, with over a third saying they should have to wait more than four years or never be given access compared to 23 per cent of people on higher incomes who hold this view.[75]

'I think the problem with the benefit scheme is everyone is a bit cynical about it now. So immediately when anyone says anything about benefits I think, "no I don't want to pay any more tax."' (Voter, London)

Policies on welfare

The British welfare system is in a troubling state. It continues to enjoy support from the public, but there are cracks both in its provision and in public confidence that it is fair and equitable. The welfare budget was seen by the 2010-15 coalition government as a route to drive down public spending, but there is limited room for further savings by continually extracting from a relatively small part of the expenditure. There are also signs that the safety net the welfare state was intended to be is now under serious strain, with delays before people receiving benefits they are entitled to, and even those who do receive support saying they are struggling on the comparatively small amounts. Despite much more stringent medical assessments for people with disabilities, the gap in employment between those who have a disability and those who do not is not closing. Without tackling the underlying drivers of the benefits bill, such as barriers to work, lack of skills and opportunity, high housing costs and low pay, cuts are unlikely to be effective on their own. Moving people off welfare doesn't necessarily mean they enter work, and can place additional demands on public services such as A&E and mental health services. Experiences of the people who receive benefits show that it can mean their incomes are volatile or reduced due to policy changes, and in the worst cases, people report feeling their personal confidence being eroded. This is not surprising given that people have to prove their incapability for work to receive a higher level of benefits.

The result of an effective welfare system should be that people minimise their time out of work through the right combination of incentives and opportunity, and there is sufficient provision for people who can't work due to health, disability or caring. In addition, there need to be opportunities where people can make a contribution even if not through paid work. More people are going to be living longer with mild to severe health conditions, and government policy needs to face up to the reality of changes in the population. Yet welfare is costing as much as it did before the cuts programme,[76] and not delivering the significant shift in employment outcomes it ought to for the investment. Even the architects of recent welfare reform admit that it will not achieve what it set out to, despite Universal Credit being fully rolled out in 2022. From the perspective of the new working class, a heavy price is being paid for a system that appears not to be working very well for those who use it, pay for it, deliver it or who have to make policy for it. It is time for a rethink on the purpose of social security in the 21st century, and to move to a system that delivers it.

Policy 1. Benefits and employment services should be based around the goal of improving earnings.[77] All incentives – financial and personal – should be geared towards enabling the individual to move into paid, sustained work that over time increases their earnings. Reward structures for Jobcentre Plus staff teams could be introduced to incentivise earnings over time rather than the amount saved on moving people off benefits. People living on low incomes are often already under stress and at reduced psychological capacity[78] to undertake complex and ultimately punitive process compliance, and therefore benefits and employment centres should use behavioural insights to ensure people can fully engage with support.[79]

> 'I've had various jobs over my lifetime and paid into the system. Benefits that I should be receiving have not come through. I have a heart condition and am no longer fit to work – this is supported by scans and tests but the benefits department doesn't listen. My arrears are building up and I could become homeless. I'm struggling to buy food and I am not getting the help I need. The culture of kindness and giving to one another is missing here. The British government don't get it.' (Voter, Birmingham)

Unemployment benefit is currently set at £73 per week. According to the Joseph Rowntree Foundation, this is a similar level to living in destitution.[80] The welfare state has long since passed the point at which welfare on its own could guarantee a life free from relative income poverty, and there is no public appetite for highly redistributive policies. Given the prevalence of low pay, the setting of benefit levels needs to be finely tuned to ensure that they do not dis-incentivise people from taking up paid work. However, the amounts people have to live on when they lose their job feel insufficient for people who have contributed to the system from previous earnings. Successive policies have weakened the contributory elements of the benefits system, and there is a case for restoring the principle of contribution as a means of meeting expectations and restoring confidence in its fairness.

Policy 2. Introduce a lower and higher rate of unemployment benefit, so that those who have made contributions through previous earnings receive a greater entitlement than those who do not have previous contributions. Demos suggests keeping a lower rate fairly basic around the current rate, but increasing the upper rate (in 2013, they suggested £94.14 compared to a lower rate of £71.70), and recommends putting the disability rate on a par with the higher rate.[81] A stronger element of contribution in welfare would allow a lower rate to be paid to entitled new entrants, while not pushing people into destitution, bringing the British welfare system more in line with its European counterparts. A bigger shift than this towards a contribution-based system would leave more holes in the safety net than we have now, so any alteration needs to be finely calibrated, but a move in this direction could help restore the public's confidence that they will receive support should they lose their job or fall ill, as well as ensure there is basic provision in place.

One of the most perverse aspects of the current welfare set-up is the treatment of people with disabilities and those with health conditions that inhibit their ability to work. Most people with disabilities can and want to work, but may need adjustments to be made to work to allow them to participate. Primarily this needs to be addressed through employer action to encourage greater equality and inclusion, including increasing the availability of high-quality part-time jobs rather than through the benefits system. Some people have more challenging conditions that make regular work more difficult, and some have fluctuating conditions that can be difficult for employers to manage if it requires long periods not working. In time, more and more people are going to be able to live well with health conditions, and most people want to work if they can. In addition, many people with disabilities and health conditions have skills and experience that go unused in the labour market due to a lack of flexibility, such as by providing peer support to others.

Policy 3. Unemployed people, people who are disabled or with caring responsibilities should be able to earn benefit top-up through a bank of flexible paid work placements. People should be encouraged to take up good work placements such as peer support networks, to enable the development of skills and esteem, whether they end up in the regular labour market or not. The top-ups should be paid for via the benefiting contractor, for example, the local authority service provider and a state subsidy, and be no less than the statutory National Living Wage at point of receipt by the individual. Improving self-advocacy should be a key part of an integrated health and employment approach (see Chapter 4).

An economy that works for the new working class

If work and the economy are going to be made to work better for the new working class, and policies to appeal to them are to be identified, it requires a shift in policy substance. In their own ways, both the Conservatives and Labour have been nudging in this direction, but they have been stronger on the rhetoric than the reality of policy commitments, or on delivery in practice. Theresa May's pitch of 'An economy that works for everyone' was precisely the kind of tone that this agenda speaks to. The problem is that there is little substance to the slogan. George Osborne appeared committed to a Northern Powerhouse, but having only launched it three years after he announced austerity, it had neither the time to get going nor the public spending commitments behind it to feel meaningful. Ed Miliband was getting at something with the energy price freeze policy pledge, but a speech was as far as that got. The consequence for voters of the new working class is that they are unconvinced that any of the main parties speak for their concerns.

Work and the economy provide a number of opportunities for symbolic policies to demonstrate to the new working class that the political party is on their side. After all, voters' social and group identities play a significant role in determining party or candidate preference, therefore parties can't simply expect voters to follow behind policies that appear to be in their interests. One of the difficulties with social class today is the lack of collective class identity, and one of the ways to define this is against another class. However, there is little evidence that class agitation has any effect on galvanising the kinds of numbers of the new working class that a political party seeking a parliamentary majority requires. The failed 'toff-bashing' Labour campaign against Edward Timpson in the Crewe and Nantwich 2008 by-election ought to have proved that elite class war does not mobilise the masses. Yet in the policy set of work and the economy are a range of signifiers a party could choose from to demonstrate their affiliation with the social identities of the new working class.

What does the attitudes data suggest would be popular policies? A new jobs and growth deal for regional England, Scotland and Wales; British business first; day one employment rights for all; a social contract for business that invests locally; a contribution-based system for the unemployed; routes into tech apprenticeships; a second chance career fund; work that fits with home and family life.

Most of this is bread-and-butter basics, and much of it not original to this book, as many of these are policies advocated by others. But the values of the new working class – and the general public at that – of family, fairness, hard work and decency – run through these initiatives. There is little appetite for total subservience to market forces, or for major income redistribution via tax and benefits, but there is an opportunity to forge a new programme based on these values for which the electoral dividend could be decisive.

6

Homes, immigration and crime

'Everyone should have the chance to save up for a deposit or a mortgage – no matter what job they do.'
(Voter, Rhyl)

The topics in this chapter all touch on something visceral for voters. And more than other topics, responses seem highly instinctive. In Chapter 3 we saw how social psychology can help political parties understand that if first responses are informed by intuition and emotion, appealing to someone's apparent economic self-interest will, in some cases, fail to strike a chord with voters. It can also help explain why two people of otherwise shared values can completely miss where the other is coming from on an issue like homes or immigration, because views on these topics can be disproportionately informed by emotional reaction. This is not in any way to suggest that a response driven by emotion is somehow inferior to reason. We are all, regardless of educational level or class or income, emotional as well as rational beings. But it does mean that political parties need to recognise that when it comes to people's homes and their communities, instinct will play a significant role. It should also help them understand that their reactions, and those of their supporters, are also in part intuitive, and that believing they are 'superior' rational beings because they think they make the better argument is unlikely to win votes.

Take, for example, Inheritance Tax, a duty paid on death on estates worth over £325,000 (as of 2017). Although most people will never pay it, it would actually be in the vast majority of the country's economic interests for it to at least be maintained, if not increased, and redistributed to other causes such as healthcare. However, voters of all incomes and classes are generally opposed to the tax and any plans to extend it.[1] Taken together with public reaction to the proposal in the 2017 Conservative manifesto for social care fees to be paid on estates at death, it is safe to assume that voters view the home and the wealth that has been accumulated as deeply personal. Although it is beyond the scope of this book to identify the proven connection between these issues and emotions, it is reasonable to suppose that people's innate instincts of security, whether through the home or in the community, group identity and competition for scarce resources, somehow come into play at certain moments on these topics. Politicians cannot avoid them, so they need to know how to deal with them. And if they get the tone, values, moral foundations and policies in tune with voters, they may find a way to deal with some of the thorniest political issues of our time.

From the perspective of the new working class, homes, immigration and crime also represent some of the most divisive issues. Recent public debate has focused on the tension of resources between what is called the working class but is more accurately the traditional working class, and recent migrants. However, it is important to note that the new working class is a much more diverse mix of social identities and groupings, which includes but goes beyond the traditional working class. It also includes what the GBCS classifies as the 'precariat' and emerging service workers, and both groups will contain recent and second- or third-generation migrants as well as British-born people of all ethnicities. Among those will be a myriad of perspectives and experiences.

It is also important to note that there is and has been concern about immigration across all social classes and income groups. In fact, concern is slightly higher among the middle-income groups than either the lowest or highest-income groups.[2] Overall, voters are becoming more socially liberal, but continue to be tough on law, order and security.[3] However, working-class voters are significantly more likely than middle-class voters to think Britain has changed for the worse over the past 20 to 30 years, and are even more likely to think that children growing up in Britain will be worse off than their parents.[4] The perception of social problems in Britain is not confined to the new working class. All classes, regardless of income, think the next generation will be worse off than the one before it. And crucial to this is how the next generation is going to be able to afford a decent home in which to live.

Homes

Britain has comparatively high levels of homeownership, and the desire to own one's home has been a driving force behind housing policy since the 1980s. Extending the right of homeownership to millions of council tenants was considered one of Margaret Thatcher's defining policies. Indeed, it had profoundly political motivations and consequences, promoting private ownership over state assets, and enabling working-class people to accumulate their own wealth. However, the failure to replenish the stock of council housing, at the same time as rising house prices, population growth and a failure of wages to keep pace with costs, has resulted in a dire shortage of affordable housing to rent or own. In the 1950s and 1960s around 200,000 to 300,000 new homes were being built every year, yet now only 150,000 homes are built each year, well short of the estimated 250,000 that are deemed necessary.[5] Demand completely outstrips supply in most areas of the country, pushing up the price of rents and sales. New build homes are unaffordable to 83 per cent of renting families across England, even with the government's new Help to Buy scheme that was launched to promote homeownership.[6]

Far from becoming a property-owning democracy, today homeownership is out of reach for millions of people, and renting doesn't always offer a stable or affordable alternative. Moreover, property has become a form of investment, so the millions who lack property or another form of wealth may face a difficult retirement in an era of reduced generosity of occupational pensions.

For those who do rent, either from a private landlord, local authority or housing association, affordability is just one issue.

Renters, which can include families with children, experience more insecurity than homeowners. Because of the lack of social housing, resources have come under increased pressure, and existing social housing stock has concentrated poverty and deprivation within places. Lack of supply of social housing has been a bigger factor than recent increased immigration in reducing the likelihood of British-born households accessing social housing, but high numbers of migrants and changes in allocation rules have had an impact, although immigration does not appear to have had a significant impact on house prices.[7]

Figure 18: Number of homes built, 1980-2015

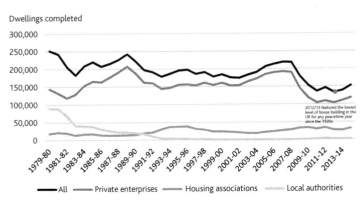

Source: ONS Digital (2016)

At the most extreme end of housing need is overcrowding and homelessness, which affects migrants as well as non-migrants, although it is predominantly people who are British-born who are destitute.[8] Even if people do have somewhere stable to live, their housing costs can squeeze the rest of their budget, making it even harder to get by. As Theresa May said in her Foreword to the 2017 Housing White Paper, 'High housing costs hurt ordinary people the most. In total more than 2.2 million working households with below-average incomes spend a third or more of their disposable income on housing.'[9] Politicians are acutely aware of the housing shortage and the impact of rising costs, although the remedies have so far fallen short of a long-term solution.

Public attitudes to homes

Public concern about housing has been rising since 2010, and there was a jump in concern immediately after the financial crisis in 2007-08.[10] Housing features more strongly when voters are asked about the biggest issues facing their local area than it does as a national concern,[11] with clear implications for local and regional politicians, which they will know if they are regular canvassers in their neighbourhoods. Housing, or 'home', is a much bigger concern for people on low incomes than for those on middle and higher incomes, and people on low incomes say they feel less in control of their housing situation than other groups.[12] Seventy-nine per cent of the public think the government has a responsibility to provide decent housing for those who can't afford it, and this has hardly changed over time.[13]

Housing is more likely to be a concern for renters than homeowners. Thirty-five per cent of private renters said housing was a problem compared to 27 per cent of local authority renters, 25 per cent of housing association renters and 11 per cent of people who owned their own homes.[14] In an in-depth study of the attitudes of people on low incomes, concerns about housing tended to be driven by personal experiences of overcrowding, precarious housing and affordability, as well as the possible threat of eviction.[15] Consistent with other studies, grandparents and parents worried about young people being able to afford secure housing in the future.

> 'The four of us in one room, isn't overcrowded and I think that's ridiculous. I think whoever thought of that needs to be smacked in the face. How dare you try and sit there and say that living in a room with two children who have to share a bed isn't overcrowded.' (Voter, London)

The public considers living in a decent home to be a right, perceives that there is a national shortage of affordable housing, and that it is getting harder for each generation to buy or rent a home.[16] They think government has a strong role to play in dealing with the country's housing problem, but lack faith in its ability to deliver the solutions needed. Historically, local hostility towards new building developments has been seen as one of the inhibitors for local and national house building, although there appears to be a shift towards support for building more affordable homes, according to attitudes polling by NatCen for the National Housing Federation.[17] It found that 57 per cent of the public are in favour of building more affordable homes in their local area compared to 29 per cent in favour in 2010, which has also been reflected in government polls.[18] Homes for social rent were the most popular choice for new builds. The reality of dealing with public opinion at the local level during a new build development can, of course, be much more challenging; however, the general swing behind new builds is a positive development for those looking for a lasting solution to housing supply.

Policies for homes

Policies for homes to win the new working class vote are fairly obvious. People want to see housing costs come down, or at least stop escalating, which can only happen by increasing the supply of homes to rent and to buy. It is how to deliver them that is contentious, and blocked by current political and legal restrictions. In their 2017 manifesto the Conservatives pledged to build an average of 187,500 new homes every year until 2022 and Labour 100,000 affordable homes by 2020.[19] But house building during both parties' most recent periods in office have been well below need, and in 2012-13 the number of new homes built fell to the lowest level in peacetime since the 1920s.

Political parties seeking to attract the allegiance of the new working class need to do more than commit to increasing the supply of housing: they need to have a plan for delivering on the promise and demonstrate the political leadership to make it happen. They will also need to take on current planning regulations, housing developers, corporate interests and potentially local campaigns against development should the public's desire for more affordable housing conflict with localised interests. Ideologically, it requires a shift in approach around public investment, and would constitute a major intervention in the housing market in the interests of citizens rather than the market. And the dividends from house building will normally be reaped in the longer term. However, short-term answers have tended to make the electorate weary when they go back to the ballot box and realise that major promises like this have not come to pass. Therefore parties seeking election need a plan for British homes for now and for the long term.

Policy 1. Kick-start a national house building programme for the generations. This should be aimed at dramatically increasing the number of affordable homes being built and transferred for public use, to help older people have good options for downsizing and release family homes, as well as property for rental, buying and part-buying. This could be achieved through a mix of legal reforms to reduce the price of land (by lifting the requirement to sell land at the highest price) and public investment, delivered through partnerships between housing associations, private developers and local authorities.[20] It will require turning some ex-industrial brownfield sites into residential communities, as well as releasing under-used greenbelt land (usually farmland) to build homes and create public spaces in 'rail corridors' around some of the thriving cites. Homeownership should be encouraged through extension of schemes like part-buying, assisted buying and 'staircasing' to increase or decrease assets according to financial circumstance, lowering the risk of eviction. Developers should be set tougher requirements to build affordable homes to rent and buy, and mixed-income communities encouraged to support social integration. Government could also require local consortia to bid for public investment for house building, and encourage the public to put pressure on local politicians to bid to increase the likelihood of public and political support.

Homeownership is an aspiration for many, but it is not a viable option for everyone. Some people choose not to buy their own home, and some cannot afford to. Renting in Britain needs to provide a much more stable form of home life, so that the households who are renting have more control over their circumstances. Not having certainty about whether you will be moved when your rental period expires, or being faced with rising rental costs, or having an unresponsive landlord – can all contribute to household stress, which fails our earlier policy of a Family Test for public policy.

Policy 2. Formulate a charter for private tenants to have reasonable protections for stability and affordability. This could include extending the minimum length of a tenancy, supported by a licensing scheme for landlords to enforce standards, and providing tenants with basic information on day one such as a written statement of rights and responsibilities.

One of the biggest drivers of the welfare benefits bill is escalating Housing Benefit. Housing Benefit has been in place since the 1930s, and is paid to low-income households to help with the high cost of renting. However, it now costs the country £25 billion a year, which represents 10 per cent of the overall social security bill.[21] Despite cuts to Housing Benefit to low-income recipients and the more high-profile 'Bedroom Tax' (where social tenants have some of their income removed if they live in a house with more bedrooms than they are deemed to need) introduced by the 2010-15 coalition government, more is spent on Housing Benefit than it was before the cuts were made because rents have risen as well as the number of renters, as earnings have fallen.[22] As we saw in the section on welfare in Chapter 5, cuts to social security are not always having the intended effect due to the reasons why some of the costs are high in the first place, so options to cut back further are limited. Ultimately increasing the availability of affordable housing is the only way to tackle the strain on social security from rising house prices, although some quicker fixes are needed in the meantime.

Policy 3. Tackle escalating Housing Benefit by re-purposing under-used housing, and link social rents to local incomes. In the absence of immediate new homes within the cities where Housing Benefit is particularly high (mainly London, but also Liverpool, Birmingham and Leeds), the Centre for Cities suggests that local authorities be given powers for Housing Benefit as well as residential property taxes, incentivising them to use stamp duty receipts to increase social housing.[23] Clearly such a move would need to be well costed and calibrated to be sustainable for the local authority as well as decreasing existing wealth inequalities. Increased devolution to cities and regions offers the opportunity to create more pragmatic solutions to housing problems.

Immigration and integration

There has been a profound dislocation between the views of the public and those of policy-makers in relation to immigration during the last two decades. For a long time during the 2000s, immigration was polling as a growing area of concern among the public, and increasingly came up as an issue on the doorstep as well as around the kitchen table. The UK experienced unprecedented levels of immigration in the period after 1993,[24] as average migration inflows rose from 200,000 to 500,000 in 2004 when the new EU member states were given full entry.[25]

Figure 19: Migration to and from the UK and net migration, 1975-2016

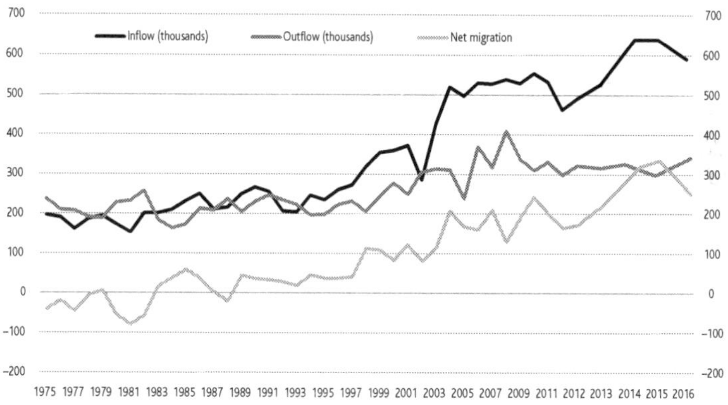

Source: Rutter (2015); www.ons.gov.uk

While emigration of UK nationals rose at the same time, net migration exceeded emigration by around 200,000 after 2004. The British population increased by 4.1 million in the decade from 2001 and 2011, and more than half of this growth was due to immigration.[26] Higher levels of immigration increased the proportion of the UK population born overseas, from 8.3 per cent in 2001 to 13.4 per cent in 2011.[27] Although among a population of 60 million, net migration of 200,000 does not appear disproportionate, population changes have been concentrated, mainly in large cities, but also in small towns, where the pace of change can feel more rapid. For example, in a decade, Boston in Lincolnshire went from being 98.5 per cent White British in 2001, to one in ten of its 64,600 population being from the new EU members of Poland, Lithuania, Latvia or Romania.[28] While many people express positive attitudes towards migrants and there are clear social and economic benefits to migration, the pace of change in some places has had an impact on public attitudes towards immigration, and politicians have not responded with much success.

During this period of increased migration, voters were caught between two dominant narratives by the main political parties. On the one hand, former Labour Prime Minister Tony Blair espoused the merits of globalisation and embraced higher immigration, and the performance of the growing economy benefited from the plentiful supply of skills as well as low-cost labour. On the other hand, his rival Michael Howard ran the Conservatives' 2005 General Election campaign on what was denounced as a 'dog whistle' slogan of 'It's not racist to impose limits on immigration', with the strapline 'Are you thinking what we're thinking?', presumably to appeal to disgruntled voters afraid of publicly vocalising anti-migrant sentiment. Howard's campaign ended in failure, and his focus on the EU and immigration was thought to further 'toxify' the Conservative brand, ushering in the era of modernisation led by future Prime Minister David Cameron.

By the 2010 general election campaign, Labour's apparent discord with many of its traditional supporters was epitomised by former Prime Minister Gordon Brown's dismissal of Gillian Duffy, an older Labour voter in Rochdale who complained about the level of immigration, as a "bigoted woman." Captured by the microphone left on his lapel for an interview, it ensured that Labour was portrayed as misunderstanding the concerns of their core working-class vote. By the time the coalition government had settled in, they were able to announce a range of measures to restrict immigration in line with the Conservative Party's pledge to bring migration down to the tens of thousands. The target has failed to achieve its goal every year, although there are indications that migration is starting to fall following the vote for the UK to leave the EU.

The consequences of this political misstep by the parties have been profound. Disquiet about immigration played a role in the vote for the UK to leave the EU in 2016. Some EU migrants are now leaving the UK, and many who remain have spent the period after the referendum uncertain of their status. Businesses and public services are concerned about the impact of a loss of all skills of migrants who have become crucial to their operation. And reported hate crimes rose in the immediate aftermath of the referendum to leave the EU. There is a certain class dimension to the immigration question because the perceived and actual benefits have been experienced unevenly. It is workers on the lowest pay who might perceive a detriment to their wages or job competition, even though the impact on wages is slight, and migrants tend to go where there are plenty of jobs. Dispersal of asylum-seekers has been concentrated in areas of high unemployment, and they are sometimes prevented from earning due to their status, meaning they have no choice but to rely on state support. More than anything, social class is played out most strongly in the way that immigration intersects with perceived access to resources, particularly health, education, welfare and housing.

The vote to leave the EU shone a light on Britain's changing social cohesion. Voters in areas of high immigration and high ethnic diversity were, in fact, more likely to vote Remain than voters in areas of low immigration and low ethnic diversity. It is areas where the pace of change due to immigration has been more rapid that were more likely to vote to leave the EU, implying that it is the rate of change rather than immigration itself that is relevant.[29] More recently, concerns about the uneven integration of migrants, new and longstanding, have been brought to the fore, and in 2015, former Prime Minister David Cameron and Home Secretary Theresa May asked the then head of the troubled Families' Unit, Dame Louise Casey, to undertake a review into integration and opportunity in isolated and deprived communities.

Reporting in 2016, Dame Casey found that alongside serious economic and social inequality, there were also high levels of social and economic isolation in some places. She commented that while there was a sense that people from different backgrounds got on well together, at a general level in our society, 'community cohesion did not feel universally strong across the country.'[30] To those living in highly integrated, ethnically mixed communities, this finding may have come as a surprise. However, to many communities across the UK with high levels of deprivation and segregation, this finding reflects their local experience. Given the UK has experienced one of the highest waves of immigration, which may have now peaked, the newly opened debate offered the chance for politicians and communities to learn from integration in the past to secure a more stable Britain for the future.

> 'It would be good to have a job where I could work from home. Not necessarily self-employed, just at home. Then I could be there for the kids and the veil wouldn't matter.' (Voter, Oldham)

Public attitudes to immigration and integration

There is and has been concern about immigration across all social classes and income groups for a relatively long period, although there are signs that this may have been overtaken by other issues.[31] Concern about immigration is relatively high across the board, and is certainly an issue for people on low incomes, although concern is slightly higher among the middle-income groups than either the lowest or highest.[32] During 2002-14 the British public has become more positive about the benefits of immigration, but is divided on the perceived economic impact, and is one of the less positive countries in Europe about the cultural impact of immigration.[33]

During the same period, the public has become more positive about accepting minority ethnic migrants, as well as more selective about who should be allowed to come to Britain.[34] Eighty-seven per cent feel that being able to speak English is important, up from 77 per cent in 2002; 84 per cent say a commitment to the British way of life is important, and 81 per cent say having skills the UK needs is important.

The public is more positive about student migrants and skilled professionals than unskilled labourers or family migrants. Unskilled workers are much less likely to see positive benefits to migrants than higher service workers, and the gap between their views got bigger between 2002 and 2014, from 23 to 30 percentage points. Those who are in professional or managerial jobs are much more likely to support migration from poorer countries outside Europe (54 per cent compared to 36 per cent of unskilled workers), poorer European countries (61 per cent compared to 45 per cent) and of different ethnic groups as the majority population (67 per cent compared to 51 per cent of unskilled workers). The public is not just divided on immigration by occupational class, but by age, education and heritage – for example, UK residents born abroad are much more likely to be enthusiastic about migration than those born in the UK to UK-born parents.

> 'I think two Polish ladies looking and there was only, I don't know, two places, and Shelly never got a place because the two Polish kids got a place because they were nearer the school and that kind of did piss me off.... I was like, well it sounds really awful, well I was like "that's not fair."' (Voter, London)

Immigration is the issue people say they overwhelmingly cannot do anything to make a difference about, and people on low incomes are even more likely to say they cannot do anything to improve it.[35] Immigration was the foremost issue for people on low incomes interviewed for an in-depth qualitative study by NatCen, although this can, of course, be dependent on context, and would vary from area to area. Respondents made the connection between immigration and other areas of concern like health, housing, welfare and education. Migrants, refugees and asylum-seekers were referred to interchangeably. People discussed feeling as though immigration was making it harder to access public services for themselves and their family, and to a lesser extent, they felt migrants received preferential treatment and unlimited access to public services.[36] Concerns were also raised about the effect on school places from local immigration, and the perception that teachers' attention was being dominated by non-English speakers.

NatCen found that the common thread in individual narratives was that immigration would cause overcrowding and intensify pressure on public services. A separate study on a town in the East of England found that over time narratives about immigration had shifted after 2005 away from asylum-seekers (the numbers of which had risen in the 1990s) and on to resource competition, perceived social impact and distrust in government.[37] From the perspective of migrants themselves, a majority say they have found Britain a welcoming place, yet a minority find they are vulnerable to exploitation and hostility.[38] A large majority of the public would like to see immigration reduced, and a significant number want immigration stopped altogether for a few years.[39] While these views are slightly stronger among working-class voters, it is striking that those on middle to higher incomes are also nearly as wary about levels of immigration.

Lord Ashcroft Polls attempted to categorise attitudes to immigration among the British public, identifying seven different categories ranging from the 'hostile' to the 'multiculturalists'.[40] He suggested that 16 per cent were hostile to all aspects of

Figure 20: Those saying immigration is among their current concerns, according to income

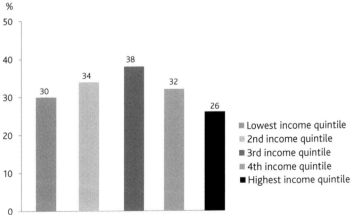

Source: Taylor et al (2017, Figure 3.2)

immigration, with the rest divided between those who were concerned about local cultural changes and the impact on public services or competition for jobs, and those who were balanced to positive. Given the socially fractious nature of the debate about immigration, it is useful to break down the constituent parts of the electorate and acknowledge that very little of the apparent apprehension about immigration levels is based on outright hostility to migrants, although that does, of course, play a part. One area of interest has been what the views of more established migrant communities have been towards new arrivals. The Runnymede Trust found that the overseas-born population were generally very positive about the cultural impact of migration, as were Black, Asian and minority ethnic people.[41] While they found that black Asian and minority ethnic people shared some concerns about immigration, they were also concerned about the impact of 'hostile environment policies' on them.

Policies on immigration and integration

The vote to leave the EU has fundamentally changed the debate and reality about immigration into the UK. Membership of the EU and the strong performance of the UK economy were drivers of the higher period of migration that was experienced during the previous 20 years, and it is possible that net EU migration will drop to a lower level year-on-year in the near future. Having said that, the movement of people is a permanent feature of an open society, and it is also possible that continuing instability in the world will result in periodic flows of refugees and asylum-seekers. The UK badly needs a sensitively managed approach to immigration that respects the wishes of its citizens but avoids divisive policies and language that can exacerbate social and racial tensions. All communities, rich or poor, migrant or not, bear the brunt of ill thought-out attempts to pacify anxiety about immigration, and too often a dog whistle or a megaphone has been used when direct dialogue would be preferable.

A range of measures has now been put in place to position levels of immigration at a more moderate level, and only time will tell whether these have been effective. Leaving the EU does provide the UK with the opportunity to set the terms of immigration policy, and delivering a more managed approach will be an important issue for the many millions who voted for Britain to leave the EU. Central to gaining public support, including that of the new working class, is ensuring that immigration policy is more in line with skills needs, and that central government is better able to match skills with shortages or areas for growth. Government also needs to demonstrate that it is investing in the development of skills of the workforce in Britain, which was a key policy in Chapter 5. At the same time, migrants play a vital role in the British economy and businesses, as well as in public services, and all sectors need to be able to hire and retain staff from around the world who contribute to the economy and society.

Policy 1. Introduce a points-based system for EU and non-EU migration once Britain leaves the EU. Annual sector-based quotas and a work permits scheme would allow governments to work with employers to ensure they have the workforce they need. Terms and conditions between agency workers and permanent staff should be fully equalised, ending what is known as the Swedish derogation that allows agency workers to be paid less than permanent staff than if they had been recruited directly by the employer, meaning lower pay for the agency worker and the risk of undercutting the wages of the permanent workforce. The government should also use the new contributory element of unemployment benefit (see Chapter 5) to bring entitlement more in line with our European counterparts.

> 'Immigrants need to be better integrated into our communities, some areas have become immigrant-only areas.' (Voter, Clacton-on-Sea)

The longstanding challenge Britain has now on immigration, aside from the immediate terms and impact of leaving the EU, is how to better integrate the migrants who have settled and those who will come. One of the major criticisms to be made of government approaches to immigration is the lack of planning and understanding of the needs of migrants and the communities they settle in. A Migration Impact Fund was announced in 2008 but was ended in 2010, and was not deemed sufficient to meet the demands of local areas having to cope with a diversity of need in education, health and other services. It is estimated that 863,000 people in England and Wales do not speak English well or at all, and in parts of some UK cities nearly one in ten of the population does not speak English.[42] Not speaking English is associated with worse health and employment prospects, as well as exacerbating social isolation and segregation. Fostering a sense of belonging means not just targeting or singling out particular minority or faith groups, but positive community relations across society.

Policy 2. Provide a new focus on social integration and managing the impacts of migration. Introduce an integration impact fund to assist local authorities with the impact that increased migration could have on public services such as schools or health, and to promote local integration policies. The All-Party Parliamentary Group (APPG) on Social Integration suggests this is funded by a levy on employers heavily reliant on economic migrants.[43] Economic migrants could be tested on their English language skills as part of their applications. As part of the skills package for adult learners (see Chapter 5), English as a second language could be compulsory for those migrants, refugees and asylum-seekers who are in good enough health to undertake learning if courses are made freely available. Politicians can play their part in rhetoric as well as on policy by neutralising inflammatory language about immigration, and supporting a new drive towards social, cultural and economic integration of all communities.

For a long time it felt to many observers as though Britain was at ease with itself as a nation, confident with its identity and place in the world. The vote to leave the EU has revealed a much more divided nation than was previously acknowledged, with sharp differences in outlook according to age, place and perspective. It is fair to say that most of the political class was in utter shock about the referendum result, and it is worth remembering that the majority of the Conservative Cabinet backed the Remain campaign along with most of the political and business establishment. Since then, many people have been trying to grapple with what the vote means and how to respond.

There is a danger that Britain could lurch into a backwards-looking nationalism, which somehow looks hostile to foreigners. For the new working class, that kind of social division is toxic.

Policy 3. Articulate an inclusive, integrated and tolerant vision for Britain, based on a set of British values that put rule of law at the centre. Dame Casey suggested teaching British values in schools, an integration oath on arrival for immigrants and to ensure British values such as respect for rule of law, equality and tolerance are enshrined in principles of public life, developing a new oath for holders of public office. Communities should be part of contributing to setting British values rather than politicised by ministers, to include the experience of minorities as part of the general public. Schools can be vital components of a new approach to integration as contact with young people from different backgrounds promotes better understanding and more positive views, less anxiety and prejudice, and inter-ethnic contact and networks can improve employment prospects.[44] Becoming a British citizen should be a celebratory event, welcoming British values, democracy, rule of law and tolerance.

Crime

Levels of crime in the UK are lower than the spike in the mid-1990s, so it has become less of a feature in public policy debate as well as in the minds of voters. There was a long period where crime was a central part of domestic policy, when opposition leader Tony Blair made one of the effective uses of the moral foundations by the left 'when he said, if elected Labour, would be tough on crime, tough on the causes of crime.'[45] In that one phrase he managed to trigger fairness (not cheating) and loyalty (not betrayal), and summed up that the New Labour brand stood for law and order as well as social reform. Since then crime has generally fallen to lower levels, and concern has steadily lowered. Concerns about crime and security can be especially sensitive to context. A rise in crime or perceived crime, or an actual or perceived threat to national security, could quickly change the priority voters place on crime and security policies. In periods of relative calm, we can take for granted that feeling safe is a given. Yet a threat to national security, as we have seen in the terrorist attacks in Manchester and London in 2017, can destabilise people. In a context of wider political or economic uncertainty, the effect of feeling that the nation's security is in jeopardy can start to erode norms of law and order. It can also quickly shift the parameters of the public's expectations of public policy. Political leadership is tested in uncertain times, and today's leaders need to be ready to provide the public with certainty and reassurance, should crime and security rise as an issue.

The crime problem as it exists in Britain today is concentrated, and once again, the new working class is more likely to experience crime than those on higher incomes. The Home Office says that 41 per cent of all property crime (excluding vehicles) is focused on just 2 per cent of the population. Adults who live in a household where income is less than £10,000 are 53 per cent more likely than the average person to be a victim of violence, robbery or theft. Children aged 10 to 15 who live in social housing are 37 per cent more likely to be a victim of violence than the children of owner-occupiers.[46] So while overall public concern about crime may have fallen, for certain people living in certain places, crime is a much bigger problem. It has a clear link to income and class, although this will depend on local context, and so crime is as much an issue for local and regional politicians as it is for national politicians.

Public attitudes to crime

Concern about crime has fallen from a high in 2007 of 55 per cent of the public citing it as an important issue compared to 10 per cent in 2017.[47] People on lower incomes are more likely to see crime as an issue than the general public,[48] which is no surprise given the concentrations of criminal activity. Over a third of people on low incomes identify crime as an important issue; however, when polled in 2015, only around 5 per cent said it was the main issue they were concerned with.[49] Crime in the local area was identified as a current concern for 23 per cent of lowest income respondents in the BSA 2017, which is higher than for people on middle to higher incomes, but is behind personal finances, health, caring for your family or another person, immigration, work and education in their list of priorities.[50] Crime and policing was more likely to feature as an issue that came up for low-income voters when they were interviewed in depth than in quantitative polling in the context of an outer London borough.[51] Anti-social behaviour was thought to have increased, and those living on housing estates talked about longstanding issues with drug-dealers, knife crime and the presence of paedophiles in the area. Older people were concerned about crimes committed by young people, particularly gang-, knife- and drug-related crime. People said they had noticed a reduced police presence on the streets, but not that they felt less safe or had experienced more crime directly.

The British public is comparatively illiberal on questions of law and order, and less than half the public express a liberal view in response to all questions on civil liberties.[52] Sixty per cent of voters polled for YouGov agreed with, 'There is never any excuse for breaking the law and those that do so deserve punishment rather than sympathy', and C2DE voters were slightly more likely to agree with this statement (63 per cent).[53] Just 19 per cent agreed that 'People that commit crime are often victims themselves, for example, many have suffered a difficult upbringing, and we should be sympathetic towards them' (15 per cent C2DE).

Opinions about the death penalty have softened over time, and now a majority oppose it. This is consistent in every income category apart from the second income quintile, which still supports the death penalty by a small margin of 53 per cent.[54] People who perceive themselves to be working class are more likely than those who see themselves as middle class to support the death penalty for those who kill police officers;[55] however, there is not as strong a differential between classes and incomes as might be supposed given education and ideological leanings. There is widespread public support for a strong state on crime and security, with half the public (53 per cent) supporting being able to detain people indefinitely without trial during a time of a suspected terrorist attack.[56] Eighty per cent of the public think the government should have the right to monitor people by video in public areas; 70 per cent support stop and search at random during times of terrorist attack; 77 per cent think the government should be able to tap people's phone conversations; and 50 per cent agree with the right to monitor emails and information exchanged on internet.

People who identify immigration as a current concern are more likely to support government interventions like those aimed at tackling terrorism, but concern about crime in the area is not associated with increased support for these kinds of interventions.[57] During the period 2002-14, the public became more positive about the impact of immigrants on crime, and fewer people think immigration makes crime worse than they used to; however, half the population still think immigration worsens crime.[58] Consistent with the relatively illiberal views of the public on crime and security, voters of all classes chose their top two policy preferences from a given list of 'amending human rights law to ensure the swifter deportation of criminals who were foreign nationals' and 'harsher sentences for crimes involving violence and sexual assault,' and this policy was particularly strongly supported by voters in occupational class E and those on household incomes under £10,000.[59] The next most popular policies across all groups were 'ending the automatic release of prisoners part way through their sentences' and 'increasing the amount of police on the streets.'

Policies on crime

Crime is an area where it could be easy to win popular support, but the means by which to do so could be detrimental to the long-term security and prosperity of the nation. As Tom Gash pointed out in *Criminal: The truth about why people do bad things*[60] many of the political approaches to crime are based on myths about what works, for example, tougher sentencing doesn't reduce crime. Such a set of relatively illiberal popular attitudes could tolerate and even welcome increased authoritarian policies, particularly in a time of heightened anxiety.

Political parties need to exercise a great deal of responsibility in the way they communicate with and appeal to public sentiment, as crime and security go to the very core of people's feelings about how safe they are. What makes one group feel secure can make another more anxious and increase social dislocation. This is not exclusively about race, but it can have a race dimension. The general public may support random stop and search during a terrorist incident, but the policy, as it was delivered in London in the 1980s and 1990s, appeared to have no significant impact on reducing crime and certainly increased distrust of the police among the young, male, Black population who were targeted. Policies, language and practice on crime and security need to be grounded in evidence as well as consideration of the impact on social relationships, which ultimately contribute to a cohesive society as well as fostering community engagement in preventing and reducing crime. Politicians also need to appreciate that the desire voters have to see people who deviate from the law and societal norms be punished runs very deep. A visible criminal justice system satisfies a public need as well as a policy objective to reduce crime by demonstrating that there are negative consequences for offending.[61]

Policy 1. Increase visible policing in areas of higher vulnerability to crime. Visible police patrols can help to reduce crime if they are well targeted, and reassure the public that there is a law and order presence. To be effective, targeted community policing needs to be concentrated on the residential areas most at risk, and be part of wider organisational goals and concrete plans to reduce crime.[62] Between 2010 and 2016 the number of police in England and Wales fell by 18,991 officers (13 per cent of the total), due to an 18 per cent cut in the policing budget (policing is devolved in Scotland).[63] Crime figures have started to rise, although it is not clear whether there is any relationship between the policing cuts and the rise, as recording has also changed. If there are more national security concerns, politicians are leaving themselves even more vulnerable to accusations of neighbourhoods are short of police if there is no attempt to increase visible policing.

The introduction of 40 elected Police and Crime Commissioners in England and Wales in 2012 was intended to herald a new move towards locally accountable policing. In the first set of elections, turnout was so low that some were elected on as low as 5 per cent support of the electorate. In one ward in Wales, no one turned up to vote at all.[64] Turnout improved in 2016 with averages of 26 per cent compared to 16 per cent in 2012, but that is still low for a role created to give the public more of a say over their local policing. Decentralisation that pushes responsibility and accountability to a local level can contribute to reducing crime, so the principle of locally accountable policing is important.[65] With the increased focus on elected mayors along with powerful arguments for increased political and economic devolution, there is now a strong case for placing policing alongside other democratic powers in the English regions and Wales. A more legitimate democratic line from community to statutory responsibility could help encourage better community and partner engagement in identifying issues and problem-solving, which is considered part of an effective approach to reducing crime.[66]

Policy 2. Abolish the posts of the 40 Police and Crime Commissioners, and move their responsibilities to the elected governments in cities and regions. Responsibility for policing in London and Manchester rests with the mayor and the rest of the English regions and Wales should follow their lead. The move should be driven by the need to increase democratic accountability and effective resourcing rather than to reduce costs, so powers and staffing should transfer; however, any savings that are made should be redeployed into the area's police force to increase visible and community policing.

Leaving the EU presents an important moment for the UK to determine its approach to EU human rights legislation. In relation to crime, delayed deportations of EU nationals convicted of crimes in Britain have been a subject of public debate, and the government has moved to deport people without the right of appeal in the sentencing nation. Clearly it is consistent with the rule of law and public opinion for the British courts to determine whether criminals from foreign countries have the right to stay after a serious crime has been committed. However, denying foreign-born people the same rights of appeal undermines the British rule of law, when it should underpin our identity as a civilised nation.

Policy 3. Equalise conditions for deportation for foreign criminals for EU and non-EU migrants, but apply the rule of law regardless of country of origin so that foreign-born people found guilty of a crime are entitled to the same rights of appeal as a British citizen. Politicians need to take care that this is presented as taking a principled stand to enforce the British criminal justice system, and avoid creating an environment in which some social groupings feel demonised, which will only exacerbate distrust within communities that already feel socially isolated.

Avoiding negative consequences

Where a political party stands on law and order can tell voters a lot about it. It gives the voter clues about the moral code that the party is likely to work to should it govern the country. Therefore, parties need to be sure that the clues it wants voters to pick up about its moral foundations chime with general public sentiment, and are the ones that are intended. The mainstream media plays a particularly important role in shaping the translation of crime and community policies to the public, so parties need to make sure that their approach will resonate with the public as well as symbolic policies being exceptionally well communicated. Increasingly parties are able to communicate directly with the public as the mainstream media becomes a declining source of news, but they still need to pay close attention to public feeling and not dismiss the source of the public's sometimes illiberal views as being an invention of the tabloid media. It is likely that the political influence of the mainstream media will decline over time, but it is not a given that attitudes will necessarily shift in a more liberal direction. The best that parties can do is establish as much of a direct dialogue with voters as possible, testing policies for evidence as well as the emotions they evoke among the voters.

What works for the mainstream tabloid media may backfire for the political party among key social groupings. A too vigorous approach to community policies may win favourable headlines in the popular dailies, but it can alienate voters who do not relate to the sentiment or who feel it is an attempt to whip up a hostile environment for certain groups. The Conservatives have historically polled lower than Labour among Black Asian and minority ethnic voters, yet, despite attempts to 'detoxify' their image, as recently as 2016 ran a campaign for London Mayor that linked their rival, who happened to be Muslim, to Islamic terrorism, and issued local leaflets including ethnic targeting.[67] The signals were picked up by voters in London and the campaign appeared to misjudge public feeling. It was said to have been highly contentious within the Conservative Party following candidate Zac Goldsmith's defeat by London's first Muslim Mayor, Sadiq Khan, and senior figures such as Baroness Sayeeda Warsi expressed their disapproval.

This book is as much about how political parties build long-term allegiance as it is about policies, and elections have shown that the public does not generally reward political parties for socially divisive campaigns. The damage of such a campaign to a party or a politician can be long term. Once a negative image is in the mind of the electorate, whether it is perceived that the Conservatives are soft on racism or Labour is soft on crime and security, subsequent actions that appear to reinforce that view can undermine years of quieter progress. More than any area, issues relating to people's homes, their communities and their security need to be at the centre of political parties' thinking because of how strongly voters feel, but their interventions need to trigger the right moral foundations and avoid negative unintended consequences.

7

Democracy

"I feel I have no voice in society. I don't have a concept of my voice being heard.' (Voter, Oldham)

At its core, this story is about power. Politics, democracy and policy-making have failed to keep pace with the profound structural changes that have taken place in society over the past 40 years, and the consequent dislocation of political representation from the mass of people is undermining democratic legitimacy. The political theorist Robert Dahl described the democratic ideal as, 'In making collective decisions, the ... interests of each person should be given equal consideration.'[1] From education to immigration to housing, it is clear that the interests of each person have not been given equal consideration. Power has become increasingly concentrated rather than dispersed, and has shifted between and within groups rather than widely shared.

In every developed liberal democracy there are signs that traditional democracy is creaking. Populist movements have gained support, voter turnout has declined and fewer people are members of political parties. Citizens have become increasingly distrustful of politicians and the capacity of politics to serve them, exacerbated by recent scandals over financial expenses and harassment. There is no straightforward explanation. Corruption is low. Citizens are more critical, but this does not explain widespread mistrust. Collective expression has waned,[2] but this does not offer a full account. The reorientation of power in society and the economy has fundamentally altered who governs. Changes in social class are central to understanding these shifts in power, and to underpinning the kinds of democratic reform that would strengthen and re-legitimise modern democracy.

The decline in the political and democratic representation of working-class people is partly due to the impact of a series of economic and industrial trends. But this has not simply been an accident. It has been enabled by a systematic dismantling of working-class institutions, accompanied by the denigration of what it means to be working class. 'What I do not think many people have yet woken up to is that the working class has been subjected to a sustained programme of social contempt and institutional erosion which has persisted through many different governments and several political fashions.' The author of this? Aristocrat and former head of policy for Margaret Thatcher, Ferdinand Mount.[3]

In his book on the class divide in modern Britain,[4] Mount describes how over the past 70 years the social and spiritual places of working-class people have been degraded. The places of worship and belonging, trade unions, friendly societies and systems of mutual aid, which had been built up through the 19th and early 20th centuries, have been undermined by successive government actions. The most public of these is the series of laws since 1980 designed to weaken the industrial and political activity of trade unions, which continue to the present day. Cheered on by a hostile media, trade unions have been subjected to a sustained campaign of vilification, even though their standing among the public has recovered from its post-1970s low.[5] Institutional erosion has also been enabled by the increased marketisation of private and family life, where seemingly every pastime comes with a price tag. The most extreme example is the escalation in the price of football match tickets that has made the most basic recreational activity prohibitively expensive for many low- and middle-income families. But it is symptomatic of working-class interests being pushed out due to their unequal political, social and cultural representation in public life.

The social and cultural manifestation of the denigration of working-class institutions has become deeply personal. Daytimes and evenings of mainstream television programming are now thrown over to shows about life on a low income. But these are not told from a neutral standpoint. Reviewing one typical programme, 'My Big Benefits Family', Abigail Scott Paul wrote, 'It is hard to see any other point to the show than blaming and shaming the family that was featured in it. The Twitter reaction to it reflected a stereotyped view that poverty is simply caused by people's bad choices.'[6] Other programme titles include 'Benefits: Too Fat to Work' (also Channel 5), 'Nick and Margaret: We All Pay Your Benefits' (BBC), and, of course, 'Benefits Street' (Channel 4), which enabled the wider media to find its exemplification of the undeserving poor in White Dee, a participant who reportedly later tried to commit suicide.

This onslaught of hostile programming has been matched with a wider linguistic denigration of people living on a low income. Within the past decade, the term 'chav' has become, in the words of Imogen Tyler, 'a ubiquitous term of abuse for the white poor.'[7] In 'Chav mum, Chav scum', Tyler details the role that reactions of disgust and contempt have in sustaining social order, and in his book developing the theme,[8] Owen Jones opens by asking, 'How has hatred of working-class people become so socially acceptable?' Of course there are plenty of examples of much-loved working-class people on screen, and there are frictions within classes as well as between them. But it is difficult to escape the notion that being working class in public life is only acceptable if the individual is a fictional character in a soap opera who doesn't challenge the social order and behaves 'respectably'. This is a wider issue for all working-class people in public life, particularly if they come from outside London or the South East. Just think how the elite media mocked John Prescott for his speech and dialect. Jones concludes by saying, 'Pride in being working class has been ground down over the past three decades. Being working class has become increasingly regarded as an identity to leave behind.'

> 'There is a lovely beach at Jaywick and media portrayal was unfair. I wanted to join the community there to help. After the TV programme, houses there lost 40% of their market value.' (Voter, Clacton-on-Sea)

'Left behind' were the words that echoed around the UK's media and political elite following the shock vote to leave the EU at the referendum in June 2016. The people had been asked to endorse a view, and effectively came back with the wrong answer. To the surprise of most commentators, the turnout among those on lower incomes was much higher than expected, and a majority of them voted to leave the EU,[9] against the establishment recommendation. Nearly all of the increase in turnout came from those who reported 'not very much' or 'no' interest in politics.[10] Age and education level were more significant indicators of whether someone voted to leave or remain, but nonetheless, one of the big post-vote questions for Remainers was why so many people with seemingly so much to lose from withdrawal from the EU would vote to do so.

The answer is partly revealed in pre-referendum research by Robert Ford and Matthew Goodwin, who describe this feeling of people being left behind in their 2014 book on the rise of UKIP, *Revolt on the right*:[11] 'on the wrong side of social change, are struggling on stagnant incomes, feel threatened by the way their communities and country are changing, and are furious at an established politics that appears not to understand or even care about their concerns.' Clearly care has to be taken to ensure that this accurate description of a minority is not interpreted as a generalisation about either all those who voted to leave or all those on low incomes. It also does not represent the view of what we are calling here the new working class, which will have been more evenly split between those who voted leave and those who voted remain. However, it does offer an insight into part of the political disengagement expressed through the vote. More worryingly, it is far from clear that the act of leaving the EU will bring about the kind of renewal that is required to reconnect the mass of citizens to democracy. For serious democratic renewal to occur, politicians and political institutions should start by listening to the expressed views and attitudes of the electorate about what they actually want from democracy, to which the rest of this chapter is devoted.

Public attitudes to democracy

Attitudes data reveals that while party identification has decreased, interest in politics has increased among all income groups since 2000.[12] Overall the proportions of those interested in politics have not changed much in the last 30 years: around one-third say they are interested in politics a great deal, one-third say some, one-third say not much.[13] However, people on lower to middle incomes are much less likely to describe themselves as being 'very' or 'fairly' interested in politics.[14] They are generally less likely to turn out to vote in elections.[15] They are also less likely to say they have a good understanding of politics. Their relative lack of interest and perceived understanding of politics is driven by lower levels of educational qualifications and age,[16] rather than their financial circumstances, but the fact that there is an association between interest, knowledge and income suggests that there is a democratic gap for people on low incomes. Social status is a strong predictor of who exercises their wider democratic rights, and this gap between the 'politically rich' and the 'politically poor' may widen as democratic methods expand and demand greater cognitive and other resources.[17]

> 'I don't get involved I don't take note of it. Whether that's the right or wrong thing, I don't know, but I never have.' (Voter, London)

Figure 21: Interest in politics, according to income

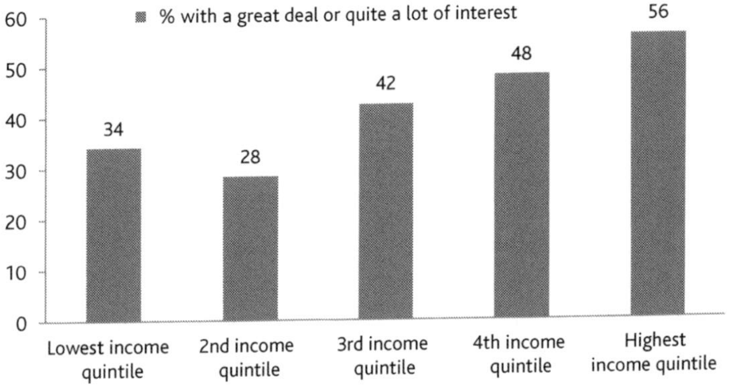

Source: Taylor et al (2017, Figure 6.1)

There is a general problem with the legitimacy of representative democracy, but this is even more the case for people on lower incomes. There is a lot to be said about how and why we got to this point, where and when voter trust broke down, but that is not the scope of this book, which is concerned with what to do about it. Around half the population agree that people like them do not have a say about what the government does. This is the case across income groups, and only slightly less the case for those on the highest incomes.[18] The same pattern occurs on trust in MPs and the government: just under a third of each income group say they never trust the government, apart from those on the highest incomes, who have slightly more trust in government.[19]

> 'You get to vote, yeah – but that doesn't mean we are heard.' (Voter, North Shields)

This is not just a picture of distrust among those on the lowest incomes, but also across all middle- and lower-income groups. Those who perceive themselves to be working class, whether in a working-class occupation or not, are significantly more likely to distrust MPs on the whole, so there is a subjective perception dimension at play on questions of trust, as well as material factors.[20] But those on lower incomes say they feel that 'the decks are stacked against them', that changes will be pursued irrespective of their views, for example, on hospital closures or schools.[21] There is also a sense that they would be the ones to live with any negative consequences. Overall, 'people on low incomes feel less in control of their lives and have less faith in politicians to act in the national interest', according to NatCen.[22] This feeds through into a feeling that they have insufficient knowledge about the political process and contribute little to influencing change, that their voices would not be heard if they did express an opinion, and a belief that the political system does not work for them because politicians serve their own interests.[23] Unsurprisingly, therefore, people on low incomes are less likely than those on higher incomes to see voting as a duty, or to have taken part in a political activity like signing a petition or attending a public meeting.[24]

The wealthier someone is, the more likely they are to identify with a political party. The data suggest the two-party electoral system is not working too badly for those at the upper end of the income spectrum, with more than 70 per cent identifying with either the Conservatives (46 per cent) or Labour (27 per cent).[25] It is sometimes said that income or class is no longer a signifier of party allegiance, which is partly true, but only in so far as Labour's support is much more spread across the income spectrum. Only about half of those on the lowest incomes identify with any political party, and they are more evenly split (30 per cent supporting Labour and 23 per cent supporting the Conservatives)[26] (see Figure 1, Chapter 2).

The 2017 General Election increased support among working-class voters for the Conservatives, but it is too soon to tell whether it is a turning point or whether it reflects the position the Conservatives took on Brexit, identity and immigration issues. Both Labour and the Conservatives increased their showing with low-income voters by 8 per cent, and analysis showed that while low-income voters were torn between concerns about living standards and identity, living standards were a stronger driver behind the vote.[27] Latest election data is, to an extent, responsive to circumstances, but the underlying trends in political leaning are more enduring. People on lower to middle incomes are more likely to be left wing (assessed on agreement with responses to statements such as 'there is one law for the rich and one law for the poor').[28] However, there is awareness of social inequality across the spectrum: more than half of the wealthiest fifth think that ordinary working people do not get their fair share.[29] There is little difference on how authoritarian people are according to income.[30] A majority of the public describe British society as being divided by class, and this is more acutely felt by those who are working class. All classes perceive that social mobility – the ability to move between classes, usually upwards – is decreasing.[31]

Many proponents of democratic reform propose far greater levels of devolution across the UK's countries, cities and regions, and advocate electoral reform of the voting system. However, there is no great public clamour for either. Support for electoral reform has increased, but is still a minority preference (27 per cent supported in 2011, compared to 45 per cent in 2015).[32] Around half the population in England want it to be governed as it is now, with laws made by the UK Parliament, although a majority (60 per cent) in England support England-only MPs voting on English matters in the UK Parliament.[33] Support for an English Parliament is slightly higher among those on low incomes, although even then the figures are low, with only 22 per cent of those on low incomes in favour (compared to 20 per cent overall).[34]

There has been a steady increase since 2010 in Scotland in support for independence, although a majority still favour the present arrangement of Scotland remaining in the UK with its own Parliament.[35] While there is little public demand for greater devolution in England, the experience of devolution in Scotland does offer an interesting insight into voters' trust in government. Public trust in the Scottish Government in Scotland is much higher than trust in the UK government (when polled in 2015, 73 per cent of voters in Scotland said they trusted the Scottish Government to act in Scotland's best interests 'just about always' or 'most' of the time compared to 23 per cent who said that of the UK government).[36] Just 17 per cent of voters in Scotland said the UK government listens to people's views before it takes decisions compared to 59 per cent who said the Scottish Government was 'very good' or 'quite good' at listening to people's views before it takes decisions.[37] In Wales, support for national independence is much less than in Scotland, although a majority back retaining the Welsh Assembly as part of the UK with current or extended powers. Research conducted 20 years after devolution found that while politicians in the Welsh Assembly were more trusted to care about Wales' problems than their counterparts in London, voters were unimpressed with the difference devolution had made to their daily lives.[38] Two-thirds said devolution in Wales had made no difference to their living standards, and four out of five said devolution had either made the health service worse or had made no noticeable difference.

The devolution of power from Westminster to parliaments, assemblies and mayors in the nations, regions and cities of the UK has been the most significant democratic reform in recent British history. Theoretically bringing democratic structures closer to people's national identity – or their city – offers the opportunity for much greater democratic connection. Yet the practice reveals a more mixed picture. While 61 per cent of voters in Scotland say having a Scottish Parliament gives ordinary people more say in how Scotland is governed,[39] this view is more likely to be held by those on higher incomes (66 per cent compared with 55 per cent of those on lower incomes).

Just 41 per cent of those with no formal qualifications were likely to trust the Scottish Government to make fair decisions compared with 51 per cent of those educated to degree level.[40] This suggests that even in a favourable climate such as Scotland, devolution of power in and of itself is no panacea for the democratic gap felt by the new working class. What matters is making a difference to people's circumstances and whether decision-making is seen as responsive to people's input. Devolution creates a broader canvas of opportunities in which to achieve these goals, but does not by itself guarantee greater political representation for the new working class. The challenge is how devolution can be fully realised as a means to the end of greater political equality for each citizen, not just a transfer of power from one set of political elites to another.

Democratic reforms

This section is entitled 'democratic reforms' rather than 'policies', recognising that while there is disaffection with the political system as it is, policies promising more power to the people are likely to sound somewhat abstract on the campaign trail. If we accept that democracy is not serving the interests of the new working class well, what should be done about it? Champions for democratic engagement highlight new forms of innovative methods to engage the wider electorate in politics. But like the policies in the rest of the book, we should start where the public is.

There are pretty clear views from the public about what they want from democracy and their elected representatives. The reforms most people favour tend to be about restoring representative democracy rather than new opportunities for participation, reflecting the fact that most people do not want more day-to-day involvement in politics.[41] This does not mean that innovative methods cannot be an enhancement to democratic engagement, if made truly inclusive. People's preference is to make those who make decisions, especially elected representatives, open about their actions and deliver what is promised, according to an extended Hansard Survey for the political scientists Gerry Stoker and Colin Hay.[42] Constitutional and institutional changes are much less frequently mentioned by voters than transparency and accountability of decision-making,[43] which is not to say they are not part of the picture, but are not seen by the public as so important. Having more people like themselves as MPs is also less prominent, as is getting politicians 'to be more normal'. People strongly favour the constituency representative, and tend to have a more positive opinion of specific politicians with whom they have had personal contact than politicians more generally.[44] Voters want MPs to represent the wishes of constituents, preferring MPs who typically spend three days a week on constituency issues and two days on national policy, and prefer MPs who speak out against the party line.[45] Other personal characteristics such as their gender or experience matter a lot less, although social identities and groupings can play an underlying association with party brands. For political leaders, voters now rank integrity as the most important attribute.[46]

> 'An ideal MP would be someone who has had a rough time and knows what life is about and has changed their life for the better and become successful. Or someone who is not judgemental and listens to everyone.' (Voter, York)

Reform 1. Strengthen representative democracy by getting the basics right and using digital technology to increase reporting back. The number one priority should be making representatives' pledges more public, explaining how policies affect voters, and showing to voters whether their representatives have followed through on their promises. Voters in Harlow suggested re-branding MPs as local representatives, to strengthen their local connection, and publishing monthly results in the local paper.[47] There should also be reform of the role of the MP, as proposed as far back as 2007 as part of the 'Positive Politics' project, such as a more accurate job description for MPs, rooting the MP more in their constituency, no second jobs, no lobbying and no perks.[48] Many MPs will hear from disadvantaged constituents as part of their regular surgeries to respond to individual problems, but their constituency offices will have to go well out of their way to ensure that the views of the new working class are sought out as part of their local democratic pushes. Representation in Parliament of members of the new working class matters too: it may rank as less important to voters, but lack of representation by those with life experience outside Westminster has reinforced a negative image that MPs do not understand people's lives.

> 'If they make promises, it should be made law. If they say they will create 500 jobs for a year it should be law that they do that, not for them to be able to say 'right, I'm in power now, forget it'.' (Voter, Hull)

Nationally elected representatives clearly have a responsibility to ensure that the views and opinions of the new working class are heard both collectively and individually as part of local democracy. The responsibility also rests at local level and within communities to strengthen the social fabric where people demand better political representation. Reforming democracy to better serve the interests of the new working class needs to be bottom-up as well as top-down. Over the course of the period that traditional political engagement and the institutions of the traditional working class have declined, there has been a diversification of the methods through which people make their views known and other social associations have been formed. Non-party affiliated activities like mass e-petition signing have taken off, mobilising people around issues rather than broader-based movements, as might have been seen in the 1960s or 1970s.

The communications revolution has resulted in a more searching and questioning citizenship, which has been seen in the developed and secure nations as well as an expression of democracy in authoritarian regimes. It is easy to dismiss the new forms of democratic engagement as individualised actions lacking collective context, not like the good old days of marches and mass movements. Yet people's voices are being heard, social bonds are being formed in new ways and institutions are responding to the demand from a more educated citizenry with innovative approaches like citizens' juries. There is also not a death of collective political activity: just look at the high political engagement in Scotland before and after the referendum on independence in 2014 (which did not happen around the vote to leave the EU, according to the Hansard Society[49]). New models of participative democracy like citizens' juries, councils, assemblies and participatory budgeting offer ways to unlock voter engagement. The risk is that social gaps may be even wider in non-electoral forms of political participation like deliberative democracy, and exacerbated unless the social barriers to participation experienced by people who are disadvantaged are effectively addressed.[50]

Institutions and emerging devolved authorities have a responsibility to share power with citizens and to do so in ways that are inclusive; but just as important is the need to promote a more enabling environment for people's self-organisation. The workplace does not have to be the primary locus of empowerment. Trade unions have already branched out into non-traditional mobilisation such as Unite's community membership that brings together people from across society, or innovative approaches like IndyCube, which is part office space, part union and part cooperative.[51] Community Land Trusts have expanded in the last few years, where local people run and manage land and housing for the public benefit. WorkerTech has been launched to support practical ideas for workers in the gig economy (workers employed on short-term and freelance contracts) to collectivise and improve conditions through shared technology. Unless the institutions of the new working class are formed or re-formed, the opportunities afforded by greater devolution of power to improve democratic legitimacy for people of the new working class will be lost.

'We need an extra hand to help us interact. Currently we are not valued. The wider community needs to have meetings. If people are involved more then they will be willing to engage. It's all about voice, people, and power. We are only consulted during election time when the politicians want to win voters, otherwise it's the same people involved in the decision-making processes and politicians only move in their own circles.' (Voter, Oldham)

Reform 2. A new civic alliance should be founded around places and communities to support the self-organisation of the new working class, creating an enabling environment for trade unions and community organisations to flourish. It needs to be easier for community organisations to step into vacant spaces, and places where people can organise around non-party lines. Poverty Truth Commissions, where people in poverty are supported to come together with local decision-makers to work on improving understanding and action over priority issues, offer an example of an inclusive approach. Collective self-organisation can have a proven positive effect on the ability of people to advocate for themselves at an individual level, whether navigating public services or markets. By strengthening the self-organisation of the new working class, and nurturing its leaders, communities will be better able to respond to the promise of devolution and to participate in more innovative approaches to democratic engagement.

One of the major problems with modern democracy is that policy-making has become the convoluted business of a professional elite. Politicians often mediate policies through a wider policy network to stretch beyond the civil service, to organised lobby groups, businesses, public affairs agencies, universities and think tanks, usually staffed by professionals.[52] This is a legitimate part of democracy, but it can mean that the views of the electorate are overlooked, particularly when those views contrast with the given view of experts. The narrowness of the backgrounds of professional politicians compounds the problem: as Rachel Wolf, former adviser to David Cameron noted, the impact of policy churn in further education was unlikely to become a political issue because it did not affect the sons and daughters of decision-makers and influencers.[53] Experts and evidence have a really important role in democracy, but so, too, does political legitimacy, and when that is navigated exclusively by elected representatives it becomes problematic when they have themselves become more detached from the reality of people's lives. Decisions out of the hands of ordinary voters means they can constantly blame government for failing to live up to their expectations, whereas a new kind of policy-making that is rooted in public attitudes can help guide politicians to a more meaningful long-term programme of action that wins public legitimacy. Policy-making is far more likely to stick for the long term if there is the public will to underpin it.

Reform 3. Root policy-making in public attitudes based on deep public insight and understanding. The role of the public has been reduced to the people who vote once every few years in a usually binary choice between two candidates. Politicians and policy-makers should take a giant leap of faith and start their policy thinking with where the public is at, building their policies up and out of their opinions, using inclusive innovative methods to develop actions alongside people. Enhance traditional engagement with an assessment of what the public's view is through quantitative polling and qualitative research, which has become a sophisticated industry but thus far largely for private rather than public benefit, and by asking what the morally right or wrong approach is. Building evidence of what has been tried to date, and publishing that evidence alongside any policy,[54] is a missing link in policy-making, dooming a revolving door of

Figure 22: Public attitudes-led policy-making

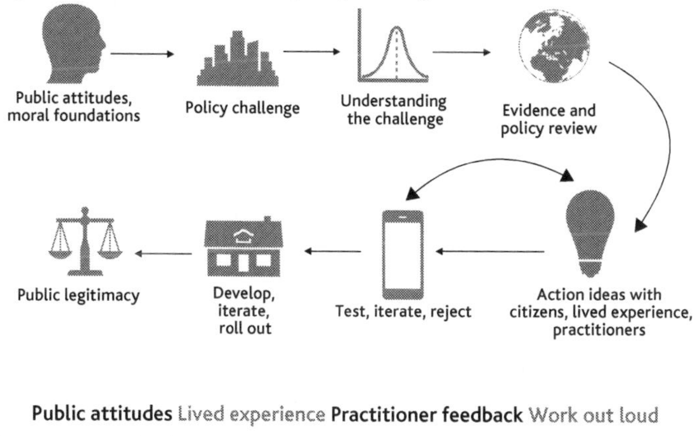

Public attitudes, moral foundations — Policy challenge — Understanding the challenge — Evidence and policy review

Public legitimacy — Develop, iterate, roll out — Test, iterate, reject — Action ideas with citizens, lived experience, practitioners

Public attitudes Lived experience **Practitioner feedback** Work out loud

Source: Ainsley (2017)

ministers to opt for the latest fad. Above all, recognising the role of people beyond their function as voter; as citizens, public service users and taxpayers, and realising that giving them a stronger stake in policy-making will only serve to legitimise the policy that results. Political parties need to be ready to listen, as well as lead, otherwise they risk just re-running the focus group model and only hearing what suits them.

Democracy for the 21st century

If this book had been written prior to the EU referendum in June 2016, the main recommendation on democracy could conceivably have been to move powers back to Britain from the EU. The data clearly showed that a majority of the population have been Eurosceptic[55] since the mid-1990s, and the desire to leave the EU altogether was even stronger among those in working-class occupations.[56] Among those on low incomes, support for leaving the EU steadily rose after 2000.[57] The considerable divide at the referendum between those on higher or lower incomes, or professional or routine occupations, was not nearly as large as the divide between those with a degree and those without.[58] Either Remain politicians, who, after all, were those responsible for calling the vote, assumed that the higher-income, higher-qualified Remainers would outweigh others, or they did not look at the data. Experience suggests they were that removed from the mass of voters they did not realise what a close call running a referendum on EU membership would be. Had public attitudes been built into political and policy-making more systematically, and had the views of those on lower incomes been taken more seriously, Remain politicians may have not taken the gamble. We will never know. But it does serve as a wake-up call to politicians tempted to seek a rubber stamp from the electorate.

Many of the answers to today's societal and economic challenges caused by the pace of globalisation and structural change seem too complex or expensive to contemplate. But the answers to this are deceptively simple. Make the existing system work better for the people it is meant to serve. It is probably not necessary to re-invent democratic methods – or at least, it is worth giving the present system a revamp before ditching it. Modern liberal democracy has a lot of flaws, but the alternatives, as often quoted, are far worse. The challenge is whether the vested interests of the political parties and current representatives could be softened to enable a more fulsome appraisal of the current democratic processes. However, much of what is proposed here does not rest on the need for interest-breaking cross-party consensus. Community and other movements are already underway, and could be funded and supported more systematically by foundations and local institutions. There is no reason why the civil service or a political party or a think tank could not begin modelling public attitudes-led policy-making, and test out the proposition that public legitimacy in policy will be heightened under these conditions. For political parties, the argument needs to move beyond whether it is in their interests to have an active and organised new working class. It is now a fundamental question of whether democracy, politics and policy-making can keep up with the society around it, and modernise itself for a new era.

8

How to win hearts,
minds and votes

Although this story started in Clacton-on-Sea and Hartlepool, it is a story about everywhere. As it seems that politics and policy-making have become distorted towards the interests and experiences of a narrow elite, somewhere the interests and feelings of a new working class have become further buried, and it is time they were brought to the fore. Although a parliamentary majority cannot be won on the working class vote alone, without understanding its needs and interests, no political party can secure an outright victory.

For all of the insightful attempts to carve up and understand changing British electoral patterns, nothing beats social class for its explanatory power in British politics. But social class is changing, and political parties need to change too. In this concluding chapter I draw together the arguments that flow throughout the book, and set out the policy agenda that arises, exploring the social and political attitudes of the new working class. As I said at the start, more than anything, this book is an appeal to the political parties and policy-makers to listen to the concerns of these voters, and to act on them.

Policies do matter, but should be viewed in the context of what and whom the electorate thinks the party or candidate stands for. While policy pledges provide the voter with important clues as to who the party is and whether it is perceived to be 'on their side', policies do have a transactional dimension, even if straightforward 'retail'-style policies can only go so far. Where political parties sometimes go wrong is in failing to tune into the emotions that run underneath the surface, but that are decisive in how our 'political brain' responds. The moral foundations theory (Chapter 3) is a useful framework for political parties to develop policy within, especially for those on the left who have historically been less effective at triggering the full range of moral foundations.

All political parties are guilty of talking to themselves too much, assuming that their ideological frame of reference relates to voters more than it actually does. A rousing speech about the evils of privatisation might go down well on the floor of the Labour Party conference, but the public are not as bothered as party activists about the means of public service delivery. Likewise, defence of the free market might be just the thing to enliven a gathering of Conservatives, but the public remembers being ripped off by an energy provider, and doesn't connect with such an abstract concept. Too often, political parties deploy a narrow set of values similar to their own, rather than reaching out to the public. Parties should root their framework in the values of the public and bridge from there, rather than start from their individual value base. Fundamentally this is what much collective working–class organisation has been about: start where people are on their economic interests and build up and out to challenge divisive social constructs like racism and sexism. Basically, parties should move closer to where the public is, rather than expect the public to come to them.

So what does a public values-based policy agenda look like? It should be rooted in the top values reported by the new working class, which happen to be shared with the general public as a whole: family, fairness, hard work and decency. The policies that have emerged that fulfil the goals of chiming with public opinion, that speak to the interests of the new working class as well as having supporting evidence, are based on a mixed economy of state, market and individual responsibility. While they position the role of the state as being the guarantor of basic services, the individual takes a more defined role in contributing to life costs. These policies require a more active business and employer interest in societal good, matching employer need for skills and favourable conditions with investing in Britain's future through schools, colleges and good work. They demand a much longer-term perspective from government, employers and citizens to meet the demographic changes of our future population, to ensure that we are a prosperous nation as well as one whose prosperity is more evenly shared.

Family

Family is the bedrock of British values. Family stability should be supported by the actions of the state and markets, and should be a central organising principle for government policy, backed by policies that support it such as putting the 'Family Test' on to a statutory footing.

An additional bank holiday could be a symbolic policy pledge, with guaranteed time off for families where both parents work weekends.

Family incomes should be safeguarded, and new state-backed guarantees on health and preschool education introduced.

Education should be re-focused on lifetime outcomes by equipping young people with the skills they need to succeed in life and work.

Fairness

Concepts of fairness need to be rooted in what the public think of as 'fair'. A key policy should be a day one employment rights charter for all, including rights such as sick pay for those who are self-employed and contract workers.

Employers should be incentivised through the employee tax system to provide job security.

The insurance principle should be restored to welfare and social care with a stronger contributory element.

Business and employers should be incentivised by the state to take on social responsibilities such as in education, skills and regional economic growth. Government should champion consumers by clamping down on excessive price rises for essential goods and services and rewarding responsible business practice.

A points-based system for migration should be introduced, which meets the needs of employers and the public alike.

Hard work

A new jobs and growth deal across England, Scotland and Wales is needed to drive a new era of regional economic growth that benefits citizens. To be successful, regional growth requires large-scale regional investment, and political and economic devolution.

Industrial policy should be organised around the goal of good work.

There should be a new focus on adult skills and learning, shifting attention and funding from higher education to employer-backed colleges, with a concerted effort on minority ethnic inclusion and progression once in work.

UK business should be able to be selected for state contracts if it can actively demonstrate its contribution to the local community.

The purpose of welfare should be to increase earnings over time, rather than simply to move people off benefits in the short term.

Decency

Policies need to be designed that enable place and community-based self-organisation to improve the self-representation of the new working class.

People want to see affordable homes via a national housebuilding programme for the generations, and making existing housing available for affordable rental.

For people with caring needs or disabilities for whom regular employment doesn't work well, a new system of flexible good work placements should be created to provide public services with skilled peer support as well as giving people a decent income, free from poverty.

There should be a new focus on social integration, respecting the rights and needs of all groups.

Racial and other forms of discrimination should be tackled head on with a new vision of respect for all.

Representative democracy should be reformed by publishing MPs' pledges and performance, re-branding them as local representatives, no second jobs, no lobbying and no perks.

This is an agenda for a socially inclusive, values-based politics. For it to be realised, a return to the notion of political equality, where no one set of interests is allowed to dominate and overwhelm the rest, is required. There is also a range of other important areas for policy that do not feature here, either because they do not appear as a particular concern for the new working class (even if they might be important to their material interests), or because they failed the public opinion test (but really should be looked at).

Intergenerational wealth, council tax reform and environmental sustainability should all feature in a socially inclusive policy set, but advocates of policy change should be aware that they face an uphill struggle to be heard. For any of these areas, the public attitudes-led policy-making model can assist by starting with greater insight into public attitudes, testing the parameters of public opinion, and walking through the evidence and options. More contentious policies, such as social care funding, need a longer warm-up than policies that already have public backing.

One of the dilemmas is whether parties should organise their identity more around the concept of Britain as a nation. This book has advocated an alternative to this. It is an articulation of who we are expressed through the values of family, fairness, hard work and decency. British national identity needs to reflect the nation as we are – pluralist, multi-ethnic, tolerant and inclusive – rather than defined against 'others'. The concept of identity comes into play on particular questions especially around immigration, and could be met through sensible policies on procurement, for example, to allow firms that meet social obligations to be favoured for state contracts.

Politicians have to be careful about how they position questions of identity, however, and attempts to emphasise national identity have too often struck the wrong tone. For example, Gordon Brown's announcement that there would be 'British jobs for British workers' in 2007[1] might have resonated for some voters, but was seen as either insincere given the perceptions of worker displacement during the 2000s, or downright off-putting to others who saw it as anti-immigrant. In 2016 Theresa May declared to the Conservative Party conference "if you believe you're a citizen of the world, you're a citizen of nowhere",[2] which was also received as an anti-immigrant expression, especially combined with her earlier comment in the same speech appealing to "someone who finds themselves out of work or on lower wages because of low-skilled immigration" for whom "life simply doesn't seem fair."

Politicians' attempts to connect with voters over the negative feelings they have about others have been pretty clumsy. They also overlook the need to organise their own identities and party brands around social groupings, and too close affiliation to negative portrayals of migrants come right up against the more socially liberal leanings of large swathes of the electorate. To some people from minority ethnic groups, moves in this direction can feel like a shift to a 'hostile environment', whatever their own views on migration. May learned this to her cost at the subsequent general election when every category of voter under the age of 50 voted against the Conservatives, suggesting that her message only resonated with older people. This gives the Conservative brand precisely the issues that the Cameron-led modernisation project was designed to address, and given the demographic changes of the future, could present real problems to their long-term electoral appeal.

This brings us to the role of positive political leadership. Public attitudes-led policy-making suggests that politicians should start with where the public is, and build from there. However, this has to be done within a framework of positive values, otherwise the risk is that weak leadership bends to the whim of public opinion, whatever the consequences for minority groupings. And what if darker times come to pass, and a nation's mood has turned ugly and hostile? It is precisely in those times that values and democracy matter most. So politicians and political parties need to strike the right balance between representing people effectively, and not being at the behest of majority rule.

One of the reasons I grouped together these diverse categories into an understanding of the new working class is that these interests have been split and separated out, the 'poor' from the 'working class', but actually there are more policies that would benefit both lower- to middle-income voters together than would divide them. They also cannot be separated out anymore: most people living in poverty in the UK are in a household where someone works. Their interests are not always one and the same, but more frequently than not, can be served by the same policies.

The recommendations here are also designed not to alienate broader public opinion, but that is partly the skill of political communication, as a shift to greater political equality means some people have to give up some of their share. Yet a society in which everyone can truly play their part and has an equal right to democratic life is something that most people will agree on.

For too long people have been labelled by others as a means to understand and categorise, whether 'traditional working class', 'just about managing' or the detestable 'chavs'. None of this will change unless there is more direct representation of people from the new working class in public life, the media, in politics and in institutions. We should call time on the deeply negative portrayal of working-class people in the media so that one day we look back on this public savaging of people on low incomes as an anachronism from a bygone era.

The final warning of this book is to the political parties themselves. Today's political parties do not have an automatic right to exist. If the voices of this new working class continue to be crowded out of public life, there is no guarantee that these new societal dynamics will not find alternate means of expression. Let this new working class come forward and speak for themselves, in a new era of political equality.

APPENDIX

Notes on the methodology

Class and income

Income and class are not the same, and there are multiple ways to define and measure them both. Definitions of class are discussed in Chapter 2, and multiple sources used including official statistics, analysis of British Social Attitudes (BSA), YouGov polling, and the Great British Class Survey (GBCS) to illustrate the definition. Analysis in the policy sections drew primarily on the BSA, and has been supplemented by other sources (such as YouGov polling by traditional definitions of social class by occupation and subjective class status) where available and relevant, as well as quotes from qualitative studies where available. While the strength of the GBCS is its descriptive depth, using it for attitudes data (even if reliable data existed) could be problematic due to uneven sizes of groupings and potential conflation with age. No primary data analysis was undertaken for the book, so all sources are referenced. Unpublished analysis by third parties used by the author can be obtained on request. All sources have been listed and attributed in the text or references, so the reader can be clear what is being drawn on and when.

There are not always distinct differences in attitudes by class or by income, and the text has made this clear where this is or is not the case. Variations in attitudes between groups tend to be subtle and have been cross-referenced where feasible with multiple data sources. One of the advantages with using annual BSA data is that the questions are asked the same way, which allows the reader to get a sense of enduring attitudes over time as they can be shaped by the medium-term context. They tend not to fluctuate much year-on-year. It is also important to recognise that class and income are not always the dominant features that shape attitudes. Class sometimes influences attitudes, and this is discussed in more detail in Chapter 3.

According to the government's Households Below Average Income survey, an individual was at the middle of the distribution in 2015-16 if his or her gross weekly household income was £483 per week; £585 for a couple with no children; £392 for a single person with no children; £626 for a single person with two children aged under 14; or £819 for a couple with two children aged under 14. An individual was in the bottom 10 per cent if he or she had a household income less than £280 for a couple with no children; £188 for a single person with no children; £300 for a single person with two children aged under 14; or £392 for a couple with two children aged under 14. The Minimum Income Standard produced by the Centre for Social Policy Research for the Joseph Rowntree Foundation estimates that 19 million households are living below a minimum income.

A technical notes on sources

British Social Attitudes, NatCen, June 2016 and July 2017; and *Social and political attitudes of people on low incomes*, NatCen for JRF, December 2016 and October 2017 (see Husain et al, 2016; Taylor et al, 2017).

These are based on income analysis of the BSA, which has been collected since 1983. The full sample is 2,942 British adults, and the data is collected face-to-face. The income analysis is a new component developed by NatCen for the Joseph Rowntree Foundation in a feasibility study in 2015, which resulted in more detailed questions on respondent individual and household income (net equivalised household income after housing data in quintiles). The BSA data on attitudes is separated by income quintiles, which is available for data collected in 2015 and 2016, following a more detailed set of income questions funded by the Joseph Rowntree Foundation to establish a more precise income variable.

The BSA uses socioeconomic classification based on National Statistics, and 22 per cent (BSA 2016, Work) of people are in semi-routine or routine jobs (a category sometimes quoted in this book). The BSA includes England, Scotland and Wales, but does not include Northern Ireland (see below). Scottish Social Attitudes by ScotCen includes Scotland-only data.

Great British Class Survey (GBCS)
This is based on a total of 325,000 online responses, although most of the analyses used in this book are from the first wave of 161,000 responses as the latter set had not been checked for errors before the book, *Social class in the 21st century*, was published. A team led by Mike Savage, Professor of Sociology at the London School of Economics and Political Science, conducted the GBCS. The material was supplemented with 1,026 face-to-face surveys and 50 interviews of those at the top and bottom of the GBCS social class scheme ('elite' and 'precariat').

YouGov/*Prospect* Social Class Survey, June 2014
Sample size: 3,245 adults in Great Britain. Respondents were categorised by 'objective' social class (occupational categorisations ABC1C2DE) and by 'subjective' status. Results were presented broken down by objective and subjective status and analysed as a combination.

YouGov/Policy Exchange survey, March 2015
Sample size: 1,771 adults in Great Britain. Respondents were categorised by occupational categorisations ABC1C2DE. GB-wide data (see Frayne, J. (2015) *Overlooked but decisive: Connecting with England's 'just about managing' classes*, London: Policy Exchange (https://policyexchange.org.uk/publication/overlooked-but-decisive-connecting-with-englands-just-about-managing-classes/).

All percentages cited in this book are based on the weighted data and rounded to the nearest whole number. Where possible, attitude data has only been cited from 2014 onwards, unless it is providing a historical comparison.

Public attitudes data refers to data collected in England, Scotland and Wales. Northern Ireland has not been included because of the lack of sufficiently robust comparable data. Some of the statistics that have been used are UK-wide, and this has been made clear in the text where this is the case.

Qualitative quotes

The quotes contained in the book from individual voters (who could be considered part of the new working class) are drawn from a variety of sources, published and unpublished including: Church Action on Poverty (2017) *Voices from the margins*, Salford; Hay, C. (2015) *What do low-paid workers think would improve their working lives?*, York: Joseph Rowntree Foundation; Hill, K., Davis, A., Hirsch, D. and Marshall, L. (2016) *Falling short: The experience of families living below the Minimum Income Standard*, York: Joseph Rowntree Foundation (www.jrf.org.uk/report/falling-short-experiences-families-below-minimum-income-standard); Millar, J. and Ridge, T. (2017) *Work and relationships over time in lone-mother families*, York: Joseph Rowntree Foundation; Patel, R. and Gibbon, K. (2017) *Citizens, participation and the economy, Interim report of the RSA Citizens' Economic Council*. The main source is the qualitative components of the BSA analysis conducted by NatCen in 2016 and by YouGov in 2017, both for the Joseph Rowntree Foundation. One quote in Chapter 2 is from 'Negotiating marginalisation: The contemporary politics of precarity', by Mike Savage, Cynthia Meersohn and Magne Flemmen, publication forthcoming, and one quote in Chapter 2 on class was taken from *The Independent*'s coverage of the *Prospect* survey in 2014 ('Threatened, isolated, under siege: The UK's working class today', a report by BritainThinks for *The Independent*, 2011).

Notes

Chapter 1

[1] 'Attenboroughisation' is a reference to the broadcaster and naturalist David Attenborough, renowned for his commentary on the natural world uncharted by civilisation.

[2] Social Mobility Commission (2017) 'Social Mobility Barometer: Public attitudes to social mobility in the UK', 15 June (www.gov.uk/government/uploads/system/uploads/attachment_data/file/618627/Social_Mobility_Barometer.pdf).

[3] Savage, M. (2015) *Social class in the 21st century*, London: Pelican.

[4] Haidt, J. (2012) *The righteous mind: Why good people are divided by politics and religion*, London: Penguin.

Chapter 2

[1] Quoted in Evans, G. and Tilley, J. (2017) *The new politics of class: The political exclusion of the British working class*, Oxford: Oxford University Press, p 123.

[2] Ibid, p 124.

[3] John Major's first speech as leader of the Conservative Party, 1991 (www.britishpoliticalspeech.org/speech-archive.htm?speech=137).

[4] Quoted in Evans and Tilley, op cit, p 124.

[5] Gordon Brown credited US Democrat consultant Bob Shrum with originating the phrase, which has been used in US, UK and Australian politics; see Bower, T. (2004) *Gordon Brown, Prime Minister*, London: Harper Perennial, p 185.

[6] Speech delivered 16 July 2016 (www.gov.uk/government/speeches/statement-from-the-new-prime-minister-theresa-may). The phrase 'just about managing' was developed by James Frayne (2015) in *Overlooked but decisive: Connecting with England's just about managing classes*, London: Policy Exchange.

[7] Additional funding available to schools for children whose families are on the lowest incomes, eligible for free school meals or certain social security benefits.

[8] Justine Greening, Secretary of State for Education, BBC Radio 4 'Today' programme interview, cited in BBC News (2017) 'Reality check: What

are "ordinary working families"?', 13 April (www.bbc.co.uk/news/education-39590198).

9 Detailed in Frayne, op cit.

10 See Taylor, E., Saunders, C. and Toomse-Smith, M. (2017) *Social and political attitudes of people on low incomes: 2017 report*, London/York: NatCen for Joseph Rowntree Foundation, p.28.

11 Ibid.

12 Sutcliffe-Braithwaite, F. (2013) 'Class in the development of British Labour Party ideology 1983-1997', *Archiv für Sozialgeschicte*, Bonn: Friedrich Ebert Stiftung, p 344.

13 Quoted in Sutcliffe-Braithwaite, ibid, citing Tony Blair in *The British Labour Party today*, p 343.

14 Abrams, M. and Rose, R. (1959) *Must Labour lose?*, London: Penguin.

15 Quoted in Sutcliffe-Braithwaite, op cit, citing multiple sources, p 344.

16 Gould, P. (2011) *The unfinished revolution: How New Labour changed British politics forever*, London: Abacus.

17 Blair, T. (2011) 'Foreword', in Gould, ibid, p xiv.

18 Evans and Tilley, op cit, analysis of British election studies, 1987-2015, p 173.

19 Heath, O. (2016) 'Policy alienation, social alienation and working-class abstention in Britain 1964-2010', *British Journal of Political Science* (www.cambridge.org/core/journals/british-journal-of-political-science/article/policy-alienation-social-alienation-and-working-class-abstention-in-britain-19642010/70E409B4E2274FAE7844449B95DA0EBB).

20 Blair, in Gould, op cit, p xiii.

21 Skelton, D. (ed) (2013) *Access all areas: Building a majority*, London: Renewal.

22 Goodhart, D. (2017) *The road to somewhere: The populist revolt and the future of politics*, London: C. Hurst & Co, p 5.

23 See, for example, Jennings and Stoker (2017), which criticises the Goodhart categorisation for overlooking the diversity of socioeconomic difference in cosmopolitan populations; Jennings, W. and Stoker, G. (2017) 'Tilting towards the cosmopolitan axis? Political change in England and the 2017 General Election', *The Political Quarterly*, vol 88, no 3 (http://onlinelibrary.wiley.com/doi/10.1111/1467-923X.12403/epdf).

24 Sutcliffe-Braithwaite, op cit.

25 Goodwin, M. and Heath, O. (2017) *UK General Election vote examined: Income, poverty and Brexit*, York: Joseph Rowntree Foundation (www.jrf.org.uk/report/uk-2017-general-election-vote-examined).

26 Padley, M., Hirsch, D. and Valadez, L. (2017) *Households below a Minimum Income Standard: 2008/09 to 2015/16*, York: Joseph Rowntree Foundation (www.jrf.org.uk/report/households-below-minimum-income-standard-200809-201516)

27 Evans, G. and Mellon, J. (2016) 'Social class: Identity, awareness and political attitudes: Why are we still working class?', in J. Curtice, M. Phillips and E. Clery (eds) *British Social Attitudes 33*, London: NatCen Social Research, p 5.

[28] Compared to 52% of middle-class voters; Kellner, P. (2014) 'The changing politics of social class', YouGov for *Prospect*, June (https://yougov.co.uk/news/2014/06/09/changing-politics-social-class/).

[29] ONS (Office for National Statistics) Digital (2016) 'Five facts about... the UK service sector' (https://visual.ons.gov.uk/five-facts-about-the-uk-service-sector/).

[30] Padley, M. and Hirsch, D. (2017) *A Minimum Income Standard for the UK in 2017*, York: Joseph Rowntree Foundation (www.jrf.org.uk/report/minimum-income-standard-uk-2017).

[31] D'Arcy, C. and Finch, D. (2017) *The great escape? Low pay and progression in the UK's labour market*, London: Resolution Foundation and Social Mobility Commission (www.resolutionfoundation.org/publications/the-great-escape-low-pay-and-progression-in-the-uks-labour-market/).

[32] Gardiner, L. (2016) *Stagnation Generation: The case for renewing the intergenerational contract*, London: Resolution Foundation, p 6 (www.intergencommission.org/wp-content/uploads/2016/07/Intergenerational-commission-launch-report.pdf).

[33] Hay, C. (2015) *What do low-paid workers think would improve their working lives?*, York: Joseph Rowntree Foundation (www.jrf.org.uk/report/what-do-low-paid-workers-think-would-improve-their-working-lives).

[34] Catney, G. and Sabater, A. (2017) *Ethnic minority disadvantage in the labour market*, York: Joseph Rowntree Foundation (www.jrf.org.uk/report/ethnic-minority-disadvantage-labour-market).

[35] Two-year average income 2013-14 to 2015-16; see Corlett, A. (2017) *Diverse outcomes: Living standards by ethnicity*, Briefing, London: Resolution Foundation (www.resolutionfoundation.org/app/uploads/2017/08/Diverse-outcomes.pdf).

[36] Barnard, H. (2017) *UK Poverty 2017*, York: Joseph Rowntree Foundation, p 27 (www.jrf.org.uk/report/uk-poverty-2017).

[37] Platt, L. (2017) 'Class, ethnicity and social mobility', in O. Khan and F. Shaheen (eds) *Minority report: Race and class in post-Brexit Britain*, London: Runnymede Trust, pp 11-13 (www.runnymedetrust.org/uploads/publications/pdfs/Race%20and%20Class%20Post-Brexit%20Perspectives%20report%20v5.pdf).

[38] Savage, M. (2015) *Social class in the 21st century*, London: Pelican, p 272.

[39] Rienzo, C. (2017) *Characteristics and outcomes of migrants in the UK labour market*, Oxford: The Migration Observatory (www.migrationobservatory.ox.ac.uk/resources/briefings/characteristics-and-outcomes-of-migrants-in-the-uk-labour-market/).

[40] Harding, R. (2017) *British Social Attitudes 34*, London: NatCen (www.bsa.natcen.ac.uk/media/39196/bsa34_full-report_fin.pdf).

[41] Marx, K. (2009, originally published 1867) *Das Kapital*, Washington DC: Regnery Publishing, Inc.

[42] Thompson, E.P. (1963) *The making of the English working class*, London: Pelican Books, p 9.

[43] Bourdieu, P. (1984) *Distinction*, Abingdon: Routledge.

44 Savage, op cit.

45 Booth, C. (1889-1903) *Life and labour of the people*; Rowntree, B.S. (1901) *Poverty: A study of town life*, London: Macmillan.

46 Savage, op cit, p 36.

47 See 'Correspondence of the Goldthorpe Schema and of the NS-SEC socio-economic classification and common descriptive terms' in Goldthorpe, J. and McKnight, A. (2004) *The economic basis of social class*, London: Centre for Analysis of Social Exclusion, LSE, p 2.

48 Standing, G. (2011) *The precariat: The new dangerous class*, London: Bloomsbury.

49 Hanley, L. (2016) *Respectable: Crossing the class divide*, London: Penguin, p xii.

50 Mark Granovetter, cited in Savage, op cit, p 132.

51 When asked 'Which two or three of these, if any, do you regard as the most important in determining someone's social class?', the top option was occupation (whether they have a 'middle-class' or 'working-class' job) (35%); how well they are off financially (30%); the sort of local area in which they live (24%); whether they went to a state school or private school (22%); the social class of their parents (22%); their views on politics and social issues (15%); their accent (9%); how they look/the kind of clothes they wear (9%); whether they rent or own their own home (8%); the kind of music, books and TV programmes they enjoy most (8%); whether or not they went to university (6%); none (18%); and don't know (10%); see Kellner, op cit.

52 Cited in Evans and Mellon, op cit, pp 1, 5; see also McKay, S. and Simpson, I. (2016) 'Work', in J. Curtice, M. Phillips and E. Clery (eds) *British Social Attitudes 33*, London: NatCen Social Research, p 5.

53 Evans and Mellon, op cit.

54 Ibid.

55 Ibid.

56 See Savage, M., Meersohn, C. and Flemmen, C. (2018: forthcoming) 'Negotiating marginalisation: The contemporary politics of precarity'.

57 Evans and Mellon, op cit, p 26. Over the period 2005-15 the percentage of the population saying 'no' to the question 'Do you ever think of yourself as belonging to any particular class?' has varied between 48-57%. Of those who said 'yes' to the first question, 23% select 'working class' and 20% select 'middle class'. When prompted by the question 'Most people say they belong to either the middle class or to the working class. Do you ever think of yourself as being in one of these classes?', 60% select 'working class', compared to 40% who select 'middle class'.

58 Savage, op cit.

59 Evans and Mellon, op cit.

60 Social Mobility Commission (2016) *State of the Nation 2016: Social mobility in Great Britain*, London: Social Mobility Commission (www.gov.uk/government/uploads/system/uploads/attachment_data/file/569410/Social_Mobility_Commission_2016_REPORT_WEB__1__.pdf).

61 Savage, op cit.

[62] Social Mobility Commission, op cit.

[63] Ibid.

[64] Savage, op cit.

[65] Social Mobility Commission, op cit.

[66] Blanden, J. and Machin, S. (2007) *Recent changes in intergenerational mobility in Britain*, Report for the Sutton Trust, London (http://cep.lse.ac.uk/pubs/download/special/Recent_Changes_in_Intergenerational_Mobility_in_Britain.pdf).

[67] See Savage, Meersohn and Flemmen, op cit, for an illustration of how personal narratives of overcoming obstacles play an important role in shaping identity among the most disadvantaged study participants.

[68] Goodwin, M. and Heath, O. (2016) *Brexit vote explained: Poverty, low skills and lack of opportunities*, York: Joseph Rowntree Foundation (www.jrf.org.uk/report/brexit-vote-explained-poverty-low-skills-and-lack-opportunities).

[69] Cliffe, J. (2014) 'Clacton versus Cambridge: Why England's political future is cosmopolitan, not communitarian', *The Economist*, 6 September (www.economist.com/blogs/blighty/2014/09/englands-cosmopolitan-future).

[70] Jennings, W. and Stoker, G. (2016) 'The bifurcation of politics: Two Englands and a divided world', *The Political Quarterly* (www.britac.ac.uk/two-englands-and-divided-world).

[71] Richards, L. and Heath, A. (2017) '"Two nations"? Brexit, inequality and social cohesion', British Academy blog (www.britac.ac.uk/blog/%E2%80%9Ctwo-nations%E2%80%9D-brexit-inequality-and-social-cohesion).

Chapter 3

[1] Achen, C.H. and Bartels, L.M. (2016) *Democracy for realists: Why elections do not produce responsive governments*, Princeton, NJ: Princeton University Press, p 301.

[2] Goodhart, D. (2017) *The road to somewhere: The populist revolt and the future of politics*, London: C. Hurst & Co, p 62.

[3] Achen and Bartels, op cit, p 35.

[4] Brader, T. (2006) *Campaigning for hearts and minds: How emotional appeals in political ads work*, Chicago, IL: University of Chicago Press, p 183.

[5] In 1966, only 13% of voters changed their minds about the party they voted for since the previous election, but this has been rising ever since, and in 2015, 38% of voters changed their minds compared to the previous election; see Mellon, J. (2016) 'How we're (almost) all swingers now', British Election Study, 7 April (www.britishelectionstudy.com/bes-findings/how-were-almost-all-swingers-now/#.WfCAq0yZN-V).

[6] Achen and Bartels, op cit, p 35.

[7] John Bartle, writing for NatCen, suggests the 'policy mood' is like a thermostat, shifting to the right when things get 'too hot' by supporting less government activity, and to the left when things get 'too cold', signalling a preference for more spending and regulation; Bartle, J. (2014) *The policy mood and the moving centre*, London and Colchester: NatCen and University

of Essex (www.bsa.natcen.ac.uk/media/38862/the-policy-mood-and-the-moving-centre.pdf).

[8]   Haidt, J. (2012) *The righteous mind: Why good people are divided by politics and religion*, London: Penguin.

[9]   Lakoff, G. (1990) *Don't think of an elephant: Know your values and frame the debate*, Chelsea, VT: Chelsea Green Publishing.

[10] Miller, C. (2017) *The rise of digital politics*, London: Demos.

[11] Bridge, M. (2017) 'How Labour won social media clash with positive ads', *The Times*, 10 June (www.thetimes.co.uk/article/how-labour- won-general-election-s-social-media-clash-with-positive-adverts-general- election-2017-qwr6r0htn).

[12] Mattinson, D. (2010) *Talking to a brick wall: How New Labour stopped listening to the voter and why we need a new politics*, London: Biteback Publishing, p 38.

[13] Mattinson, ibid, p 282.

[14] BritainThinks (2017) 'The voters' perspective: Key insights from the campaign', June (http://britainthinks.com/pdfs/GE2017_The-Voters-Perspective_170608.pdf)

[15] BARB (Broadcasters' Audience Research Board) (2017) 'Monthly viewing by genre', May (www.barb.co.uk/viewing-data/monthly-viewing-by-genre/).

[16] BritainThinks, op cit.

[17] Evans, G. and Tilley, J. (2017) *The new politics of class: The political exclusion of the British working class*, Oxford: Oxford University Press, p 59.

[18] Kellner, P. (2014) 'The changing politics of social class', YouGov for *Prospect*, June (https://yougov.co.uk/news/2014/06/09/changing-politics-social-class/).

[19] Frayne, J. (2015) *Overlooked but decisive: Connecting with England's just about managing classes*, London: Policy Exchange.

[20] Lawrence, J. and Sutcliffe-Braithwaite, F. (2012) 'Margaret Thatcher and the decline of class politics', in B. Jackson (ed) *Making Thatcher's Britain*, Cambridge: Cambridge University Press, p 134.

[21] A social grade system of classification based on occupation. Social class A relates to the upper middle class, higher managerial, administrative or professional; B is middle class, intermediate managerial, administrative or professional; C1 is lower middle class, supervisory or clerical and junior managerial, administrative or professional; C2 is skilled working class, skilled manual workers; D is working class, semi-skilled and unskilled manual workers; and E is non-working, casual or lowest grade workers, pensioners and others dependent on social security for their income. See Chapter 2 for a discussion of occupation-based approaches to classification.

[22] Evans and Tilley, op cit.

[23] Evans and Tilley, op cit, p 61.

[24] Ford, R. and Lymperopoulou, K. (2016) 'Immigration', in R. Harding et al, *British Social Attitudes 34*, London: NatCen (www.bsa.natcen.ac.uk/media/39196/bsa34_full-report_fin.pdf).

[25] Kellner, op cit.

[26] Taylor, E., Saunders, C. and Toomse-Smith, M. (2017) *Social and political attitudes of people on low incomes: 2017 report*, London/York: NatCen for Joseph Rowntree Foundation.

[27] Kellner, op cit.

[28] Lakoff, G. and Wehling, E. (2016) *Your brain's politics: How the science of mind explains the political divide*, Societas.

[29] Haidt, op cit.

[30] Mattinson, op cit, p 12.

[31] Curtis, C. (2017) 'How Britain voted at the 2017 general election', YouGov, 13 June (https://yougov.co.uk/news/2017/06/13/how-britain-voted-2017-general-election/).

[32] *The Guardian* (2017) 'Young voters, class and turnout: how Britain voted in 2017', Datablog, 20 June (www.theguardian.com/politics/datablog/ng-interactive/2017/jun/20/young-voters-class-and-turnout-how-britain-voted-in-2017).

[33] Goodwin, M. (2017) 'European populism is here to stay', *The New York Times*, 20 October (www.nytimes.com/2017/10/20/opinion/european-populism-is-here-to-stay.html).

[34] Survation for British Future (2015) *General election 2015 and the ethnic minority vote: Summary of key findings*, May (www.britishfuture.org/wp-content/uploads/2015/05/ethnicminorityvote2015.pdf).

[35] Dysch, M. (2017) 'Labour support just 13 per cent among UK Jews', *Jewish Chronicle*, 30 May (www.thejc.com/news/uk-news/labour-support-just-13-per-cent-among-uk-jews-1.439325).

[36] Mattinson, op cit, citing Birkbeck study, p 60.

[37] Evans and Tilley, op cit, p 128.

Chapter 4

[1] Fagerholm, A. (2016) 'Why do political parties change their policy positions? A review', *Political Studies Review*, vol 14, no 4.

[2] Taylor, E., Saunders, C. and Toomse-Smith, M. (2017) *Social and political attitudes of people on low incomes: 2017 report*, London/York: NatCen for Joseph Rowntree Foundation, p 11, Figure 3.2; Husain, F., Jessop, C., Kelley, N., et al (2016) *Social and political attitudes of people on low incomes: 2016 report*, London/York: NatCen for Joseph Rowntree Foundation, Figure 2 (http://natcen.ac.uk/media/1345858/social-and-political-attitudes-of-people-on-low-incomes.pdf).

[3] For example, 42% of voters say, 'I mostly decide who to vote for based on what their policies will mean for me and my family', and this is even stronger among C2DE voters (42% C2, 50% D, 44%E). Forty per cent say, 'I mostly decide who to vote for based on what their policies will mean for society as a whole' (37% C2, 28% D, 34% E). See Frayne, J. (2015) *Overlooked but decisive: Connecting with England's just about managing classes*, London: Policy Exchange, data tables (https://policyexchange.org.uk/publication/

overlooked-but-decisive-connecting-with-englands-just-about-managing-classes/).

[4] A social grade system of classification based on occupation. Social class A relates to the upper middle class, higher managerial, administrative or professional; B is middle class, intermediate managerial, administrative or professional; C1 is lower middle class, supervisory or clerical and junior managerial, administrative or professional; C2 is skilled working class, skilled manual workers; D is working class, semi-skilled and unskilled manual workers; and E is non-working, casual or lowest grade workers, pensioners and others dependent on social security for their income. See Chapter 2 for a discussion of occupation-based approaches to classification.

[5] Mattinson, D. (2010) *Talking to a brick wall: How New Labour stopped listening to the voter and why we need a new politics*, London: Biteback Publishing, citing Birkbeck study, p 60.

[6] Frayne, op cit.

[7] Unpublished secondary analysis of BSA, NatCen for Joseph Rowntree Foundation.

[8] Taylor et al, op cit, p 11.

[9] Goodman, A. and Greaves, E. (2010) *Cohabitation, marriage and child outcomes*, London: Institute for Fiscal Studies, p 2.

[10] ONS (Office for National Statistics) (2017) 'Families and households: 2017' (www.ons.gov.uk/peoplepopulationandcommunity/birthsdeathsandmarriages/families/bulletins/familiesandhouseholds/2017).

[11] TUC (Trades Union Congress) (2016) 'Number of people working night shifts up by more than 275,000 since 2011, new TUC analysis reveals', TUC analysis of Labour Force Survey, 27 October (www.tuc.org.uk/news/number-people-working-night-shifts-more-250000-2011-new-tuc-analysis-reveals).

[12] Padley, M. and Hirsch, D. (2017) *A Minimum Income Standard for the UK in 2017*, York: Joseph Rowntree Foundation (www.jrf.org.uk/report/minimum-income-standard-uk-2017).

[13] Frayne, op cit, data tables.

[14] Greenberg Quinlan Rosner Research (2017) *Post General Election poll for the TUC: The full results* (www.gqrr.com/articles/2017/6/29/post-general-election-poll-for-the-tuc-the-full-results).

[15] For example, 52% of C2DE (49% ABC1) voters support the policy to double paternity leave to four weeks and to increase paternity pay; Greenberg Quinlan Rosner Research, op cit.

[16] Frayne, op cit, data tables.

[17] Clery, E. (2016) 'Welfare', in K. Swales et al, *British Social Attitudes 33*, London: NatCen Social Research, p 5.

[18] Roberts, E., Speight, S. and Chadwick, T. (2017) *Childcare use and attitudes*, London: NatCen, pp 13-14 (http://natcen.ac.uk/our-research/research/childcare-use-and-attitudes/).

[19] This source also found that 77 per cent of the lower income group said extra-marital sex was 'always wrong' compared to 63% in the higher income

group; unpublished secondary analysis of BSA by NatCen for Joseph Rowntree Foundation (2016).

[20] Unpublished secondary analysis of BSA by NatCen for Joseph Rowntree Foundation (2016).

[21] Swales, K. and Attar Taylor, E. (2017) 'Moral issues', in R. Harding et al, *British Social Attitudes 34*, London: NatCen, p 2 (www.bsa.natcen.ac.uk/media/39196/bsa34_full-report_fin.pdf).

[22] Barnes, M., Bryson, C. and Smith, R. (2006) *Working atypical hours: What happens to 'family life'?*, London: NatCen, quoted in Fatherhood Institute (2011) *Fathers, mothers, work and family*, p 10 (www.fatherhoodinstitute.org/2011/fi-research-summary-fathers-mothers-work-and-family).

[23] Relationships Foundation (2009) 'National Family Week 2: Weekend workers: Part-time parents?' (www.relationshipsfoundation.org/national-family-week-2-weekend-workers-part-time-parents/).

[24] Ibid.

[25] Lyonette, C. and Clark, M. (2009) *Unsocial hours: Unsocial families?*, Cambridge: Relationships Foundation (www.relationshipsfoundation.org/unsocial-hours-unsocial-families/).

[26] Relationships Foundation (2017) 'Implementing the Family Test – A review of progress one year on', p 7 (www.relationshipsfoundation.org/implementing-the-family-test-a-review-of-progress-one-year-on/).

[27] Clery, op cit, p 1.

[28] Eighty-four per cent of the public think that there is 'quite a lot' or 'some' child poverty in Britain, and those on the lowest incomes are no more likely to say there is child poverty than other groups; see Taylor et al, op cit, p 19.

[29] Adapted from Goodhart, D. (2017) *The road to somewhere: The populist revolt and the future of politics*, London: C. Hurst & Co, p 212.

[30] Social Market Foundation (2016) *Family matters: The role of parents in children's educational attainment*, p 8 (www.smf.co.uk/wp-content/uploads/2016/11/Social-Market-Foundation-SMF-Family-matters-parental-engagement-and-educational-attainment-November-2016.pdf).

[31] Not reading to a child at age 5 decreases their age 11 test score by 1.5 points; see Social Market Foundation, ibid, p 8.

[32] Clegg, N., Allen, R., Fernandes, S., Freedman, S. and Kinnock, S. (2017) *Commission on inequality in education*, London: Social Market Foundation, p 7 (www.smf.co.uk/wp-content/uploads/2017/07/Education-Commission-final-web-report.pdf).

[33] Harding, R. (2017) 'Key findings', in *British Social Attitudes 34*, London: NatCen, p 4.

[34] Ipsos MORI (2017) *Issues*, May and July.

[35] Scottish Government (2016) *Scottish Social Attitudes 2015: Attitudes to government, the National Health Service, the economy and standard of living*, Edinburgh: ScotCen, p 21.

[36] Husain et al, op cit.

[37] Taylor et al, op cit.

38 Tanner, E. and Kelley, N. (2017) *Attitudes towards 'good schools' and selective education*, London: NatCen (http://natcen.ac.uk/our-research/research/ attitudes-towards-%E2%80%98good-schools%E2%80%99-selective-education/).

39 Forty-two per cent of unemployed people, 45% of people in work, 49% of retired people and 51% of people not in work (in education, off sick etc) say secondary schools prepare young people for work; unpublished BSA analysis by NatCen for Joseph Rowntree Foundation (2017).

40 Taylor et al, op cit.

41 Tanner and Kelley, op cit.

42 Sixty-one per cent support the statement, 'All children should go to the same kind of secondary school, no matter how well or badly they do at primary school'; 39% support 'Children should go to a different kind of secondary school depending on how well they do at primary school'; see Tanner and Kelley, op cit, p 7.

43 Tanner and Kelley, op cit.

44 Dahlgreen, W. (2016) 'Fewer than 1 in 5 teachers think academies improve education', YouGov, 17 March (https://yougov.co.uk/news/2016/03/17/ teachers-critical-academies/).

45 Ibid.

46 In 2014, the Coalition government extended the provision of free school lunches from low-income children to all primary school children in the first three years of school.

47 Chambers, L. (2013) 'Majority support free school meals for infants', YouGov, 19 September (https://yougov.co.uk/news/2013/09/19/support-free-school-meals/).

48 Greenberg Quinlan Rosner Research, op cit.

49 Frayne, op cit.

50 Ibid.

51 Paterson, J. and Ormston, R. (2015) 'Higher education', in J. Curtice and R. Ormston (eds) *British Social Attitudes 32*, London: NatCen. Public attitudes data on higher education, England only.

52 Ibid.

53 Universities UK.

54 Belfield, C., Britton, J., Dearden, L. and van der Erve, L. (2017) *Higher education funding in England: Past, present and options for the future*, London: Institute for Fiscal Studies, July (www.ifs.org.uk/uploads/publications/bns/ BN211.pdf).

55 Wolf, A. (2017) 'Degrees of failure: Why it's time to reconsider how we run our universities', *Prospect*, 14 July (www.prospectmagazine.co.uk/magazine/ degrees-of-failure-do-universities-actually-do-any-good).

56 Taylor, M. (2017) *Good work: The Taylor review of modern working practices*, London: Department for Business, Energy and Industrial Strategy, 2017, p 89 (www.gov.uk/government/publications/good-work-the-taylor-review-of-modern-working-practices).

57 Social Market Foundation, op cit, p 13.

[58] DfE (Department for Education (2015) 'GCSE and equivalent attainment by pupil characteristics, 2013 to 2014' (www.gov.uk/government/uploads/system/uploads/attachment_data/file/399005/SFR06_2015_Text.pdf).

[59] Clegg et al, op cit, p 6.

[60] Social Market Foundation, op cit, p 12.

[61] Clegg et al, op cit, p 7.

[62] Joseph Rowntree Foundation (2016) *UK poverty: Causes, costs and solutions*, York: Joseph Rowntree Foundation, p 125 (www.jrf.org.uk/report/uk-poverty-causes-costs-and-solutions).

[63] DfE (Department for Education) (2009) *Class size and education in England evidence report*, p 2 (www.gov.uk/government/uploads/system/uploads/attachment_data/file/183364/DFE-RR169.pdf).

[64] Norris, E. and Adam, R. (2017) *All change: Why Britain is so prone to policy reinvention, and what can be done about it*, London: Institute for Government, pp 5, 23 (www.instituteforgovernment.org.uk/sites/default/files/publications/IfG_All_change_report_FINAL.pdf).

[65] Quigley, A. (2014) 'Maintaining pride in the NHS: The challenge for the new NHS Chief Exec', Ipsos MORI (www.ipsos.com/ipsos-mori/en-uk/maintaining-pride-nhs-challenge-new-nhs-chief-exec).

[66] Ipsos MORI *Issues Monitor* May 2017 recorded concern about the NHS at 61%, its highest level since 2002.

[67] Ipsos MORI (2017) 'Level of pessimism for future of NHS, policing and education highest for 15 years', April (www.ipsos.com/ipsos-mori/en-uk/levels-pessimism-future-nhs-policing-and-education-highest-15-years).

[68] Eighteen per cent lowest income quintile; 16% 2nd; 11% 3rd; 9% 4th; and 14% highest income quintile; unpublished secondary analysis of BSA by NatCen for Joseph Rowntree Foundation (2017).

[69] Taylor et al, op cit.

[70] The King's Fund (no date) *Time to think differently* (www.kingsfund.org.uk/time-to-think-differently/trends/demography). Figures on life expectancy inequality are from the Marmot review of health inequalities published in 2010; however, there is no comparable update. Overall increases in life expectancy now appear to be stalling. Figures on inequalities in years lived without a disability or limiting longstanding illness are taken from ONS (Office for National Statistics, 2013) 'Inequality in disability-free life expectancy by area deprivation: England: 2003-06 and 2007-10 (www.ons.gov.uk/peoplepopulationandcommunity/healthandsocialcare/healthandlifeexpectancies/bulletins/inequalityindisabilityfreelifeexpectancybyareadeprivationengland/2013-07-25).

[71] Buck, D. and Maguire, D. (2015) *Inequalities in life expectancy: Changes over time and implications for policy*, London: The King's Fund (www.kingsfund.org.uk/sites/default/files/field/field_publication_file/inequalities-in-life-expectancy-kings-fund-aug15.pdf).

[72] D'Arcy, C. and Finch, D. (2017) *The great escape? Low pay and progression in the UK's labour market*, London: Resolution Foundation and Social Mobility

Commission (www.resolutionfoundation.org/publications/the-great-escape-low-pay-and-progression-in-the-uks-labour-market/).

73 People who are disabled or caring for someone else are substantially more likely to be living on a low income than people who are not disabled or not caring for someone else.

74 *Insights 2016*, Understanding Society, Institute for Social and Economic Research, p 19.

75 The King's Fund analysis of the Department of Health's annual report and accounts 2016 to 2017, cited in Buck, D. (2017) *Reducing inequalities in health: Towards a brave new world?*, London: The King's Fund (www.kingsfund.org.uk/blog/2017/08/reducing-inequalities-health-towards-brave-old-world).

76 Curtice, J. (2017) 'Role of government', in R. Harding et al, *British Social Attitudes 34*, London: NatCen, pp 5-6; Gershlick, B., Charlesworth, A. and Taylor, E. (2015) *Public attitudes to the NHS: An analysis of responses to questions in the British Social Attitudes Survey*, London: The Health Foundation, February, p 12 (www.health.org.uk/sites/health/files/PublicAttitudesToTheNHS.pdf).

77 Gershlick et al, ibid, p 11.

78 Evans, H. and Wellings, D. (2017) *What does the public think about the NHS?*, London: The King's Fund (www.kingsfund.org.uk/publications/what-does-public-think-about-nhs).

79 Curtice, op cit, p 12.

80 Fifty-eight per cent say they would not be willing for the government to spend less money on other public services in order to maintain the NHS at its current level of service (Gershlick et al, op cit, p 20); however, it is worth noting that this is based on data collected in 2014, prior to the shift in public attitudes towards spending reported in Harding et al, op cit.

81 Ipsos MORI *Issues Monitor* (May 2017) ranks social care as a 12% concern compared to a 61% concern for healthcare.

82 Appleby, J., Robertson, R. and Taylor, E. (2016) 'NHS', in K. Swales et al, *British Social Attitudes 33*, London: NatCen, p 1.

83 Ibid, p 7.

84 Scottish Government, op cit, p 25.

85 Appleby et al, op cit, p 7.

86 Appleby et al, op cit, p 8.

87 Husain et al, op cit, p 19, panel survey finding.

88 Unpublished analysis of BSA 34 by The King's Fund.

89 Evans and Wellings, op cit.

90 Ibid.

91 Appleby et al, op cit, p 14.

92 Frayne, op cit, data tables.

93 Fifty-seven per cent agreed with the statement 'Decisions about how public services are run should be made as locally as possible to reflect the needs and priorities of local people' compared to 26% who agreed with 'Decisions about how public services are run should be made at a national

level to ensure people in all parts of the country receive the same levels of service'; see Frayne, op cit, data tables.

94 Evans and Wellings, op cit, Figure 5.

95 Gershlick et al, op cit, p 15.

96 Kellner, P. (2014) 'The changing politics of social class', YouGov for *Prospect*, June (https://yougov.co.uk/news/2014/06/09/changing-politics-social-class/).

97 Gershlick et al, op cit, p 16.

98 Forty-eight per cent of voters say 'choice and competition in public services is wasteful and does not actually end up improving services at all'. Twenty-seven per cent say 'choice in public services increases competition and therefore drives up standards, leading to better services for all.' See Frayne, op cit.

99 Appleby et al, op cit, p 1.

100 The King's Fund (no date) 'Demography: future trends', part of 'Time to think differently' (www.kingsfund.org.uk/time-to-think-differently/trends/demography).

101 National Health Service (Charges to Overseas Visitors) (Amendment) Regulations 2017 (www.legislation.gov.uk/uksi/2017/756/contents/made).

102 The average person will require social care costing £20,000, but some individuals with acute needs care costs are much higher. For those with less than £14,000 in capital and savings, the state covers the cost, but pays nothing for those with more than £23,500. This threshold is due to change in April 2020 to £17,000 and £118,000 respectively.

103 For example, a joint government departmental pilot in the New Anglia Local Enterprise Partnership area to reduce the number of people who are unemployed (www.gov.uk/european-structural-investment-funds/access-to-employment-work-and-health-integrated-services-project-call-in-new-anglia-lep-oc24s17p0818) and earlier trials integrating mental health services with employment advice (www.gov.uk/government/publications/evaluation-of-employment-advisers-in-the-improving-access-to-psychological-therapies-programme-rr826).

104 As recommended by the Resolution Foundation (2017) 'All working together: How to draw more people in to the UK labour market', Chapter 4, in *Work in Brexit Britain: Reshaping the nation's labour market*, London: Resolution Foundation (www.resolutionfoundation.org/publications/work-in-brexit-britain-reshaping-the-nations-labour-market/).

Chapter 5

1 Achen, C.H. and Bartels, L.M. (2016) *Democracy for realists: Why elections do not produce responsive governments*, Princeton, NJ: Princeton University Press, p 16.

2 Goodwin, M. and Heath, O. (2017) *UK General Election vote examined: Income, poverty and Brexit*, York: Joseph Rowntree Foundation (www.jrf.org.uk/report/uk-2017-general-election-vote-examined).

3   Husain, F., Jessop, C., Kelley, N., et al (2016) *Social and political attitudes of people on low incomes: 2016 report*, London/York: NatCen for Joseph Rowntree Foundation (http://natcen.ac.uk/media/1345858/social-and-political-attitudes-of-people-on-low-incomes.pdf).

4   Taylor, E., Saunders, C. and Toomse-Smith, M. (2017) *Social and political attitudes of people on low incomes: 2017 report*, London/York: NatCen for Joseph Rowntree Foundation.

5   Corlett, A., Tomlinson, D. and Clarke, S. (2017) *The living standards audit 2017*, London: Resolution Foundation (www.resolutionfoundation.org/publications/the-living-standards-audit-2017/).

6   Social Mobility Commission (2016) *State of the Nation 2016: Social mobility in Great Britain*, London: Social Mobility Commission, p 134 (www.gov.uk/government/uploads/system/uploads/attachment_data/file/569410/Social_Mobility_Commission_2016_REPORT_WEB__1__.pdf).

7   Ibid, p 134.

8   Ibid, p 140.

9   Joseph Rowntree Foundation (2016) *UK poverty: Causes, costs and solutions*, York: Joseph Rowntree Foundation, p 46 (www.jrf.org.uk/report/uk-poverty-causes-costs-and-solutions).

10   Extra Costs Commission (2015) *Driving down the extra costs disabled people face* (www.scope.org.uk/get-involved/campaigns/extra-costs-commission-full-report), cited in Joseph Rowntree Foundation, ibid, p 47.

11   Joseph Rowntree Foundation, op cit, p 52, based on Family Resources Survey data 2013-14.

12   Sixty-two per cent agreed with the statement, 'I am generally happy with what I have in life; as long as I have my health, friends and family I don't aspire to having more' (64% C2DE, 60% ABC1); 26% agreed with the statement, 'I am keen to move up in life, to get a bigger home, higher income and more luxuries in life' (20% C2DE, 30% ABC1); Frayne, J. (2015) *Overlooked but decisive: Connecting with England's just about managing classes*, London: Policy Exchange (https://policyexchange.org.uk/publication/overlooked-but-decisive-connecting-with-englands-just-about-managing-classes/).

13   A social grade system of classification based on occupation. Social class A relates to the upper middle class, higher managerial, administrative or professional; B is middle class, intermediate managerial, administrative or professional; C1 is lower middle class, supervisory or clerical and junior managerial, administrative or professional; C2 is skilled working class, skilled manual workers; D is working class, semi-skilled and unskilled manual workers; and E is non-working, casual or lowest grade workers, pensioners and others dependent on social security for their income. See Chapter 2 for a discussion of occupation-based approaches to classification.

14   According to the Ipsos Mori *Issues Monitor*, taken at July 2017, concern about the economy is the fourth most significant issue to all voters at 25%, with concern about poverty/inequality at 17%.

15 Scottish Government (2016) *Scottish Social Attitudes 2015: Attitudes to discrimination and positive action*, Edinburgh, p 21 (www.gov.scot/Publications/2016/09/3916).

16 Curtice, J. (2017) 'Role of government', in R. Harding et al, *British Social Attitudes 34*, London: NatCen, p 1 (www.bsa.natcen.ac.uk/media/39196/bsa34_full-report_fin.pdf).

17 Curtice, op cit, p 1.

18 Taylor et al, op cit.

19 Forty-seven per cent agree with the statement, 'Government can be a force for good...' and 35% choose 'Government should be as small as possible....' There was no significant difference between occupational social grades, although slightly more C2DEs said 'don't know' and fewer agreed with the small government statement; see Frayne, op cit.

20 Curtice, op cit, p 4.

21 Taylor et al, op cit, percentage agreeing, 'Government should redistribute income from the better-off to the less well-off.' See Figure 11.

22 Kellner, P. (2014) 'The changing politics of social class', YouGov for *Prospect*, June (https://yougov.co.uk/news/2014/06/09/changing-politics-social-class/).

23 When asked who benefits from the way the economy works and is structured, 57% of ABC1 and 57% of C2DE voters select 'People who are well off' followed by 'People who run big businesses' (54%), 'Older people' (22% ABC1, 12% C2DE), 'People who work in the public sector' (17%), 'People who are on average incomes' (6%), 'People who are less well off' (5%), 'People who run small businesses' (4%) and 'Younger people' (3%). See Frayne, op cit.

24 Shah, P. (2015) 'Exploring public attitudes to tax avoidance in 2015', in HM Revenue and Customs, *Exploring public attitudes to tax avoidance in 2015*, Research Report, 401, quoted in Baumberg Geiger, B., Reeves, A. and de Vries, R. (2017) 'Tax avoidance and manipulation', in R. Harding et al, *British Social Attitudes 34*, London: NatCen, p 5.

25 Livermore, S. and Clarkson, T. (2017) *The Brexit diaries: Engaging with the public in Brexit Britain*, London: BritainThinks (http://britainthinks.com/pdfs/The-Brexit-Diaries_engaging-with-the-public-in-Brexit-Britain_170329.pdf).

26 Kellner, op cit.

27 Curtice, op cit, pp 5, 9-10.

28 Frayne, op cit.

29 *The Guardian* analysis of Institute for Public Policy Research (IPPR) figures, in 'Transformational infrastructure for the North', *IPPR North*, 7 August 2014. Based on Arnett, G. (2014) 'London gets 24 times as much spent on infrastructure per resident than north-east England, *The Guardian*, 7 August (www.theguardian.com/news/datablog/2014/aug/07/london-gets-24-times-as-much-infrastructure-north-east-england).

30 The government spends around £45 billion on goods and services supplied by non-public sector organisations every year. NAO (National Audit Office)

(2016) *Government's spending with small and medium-sized enterprises*, London: NAO, p 5 (www.nao.org.uk/wp-content/uploads/2016/03/Governments-spending-with-small-and-medium-sizes-enterprises.pdf).

[31] Thomson, A. (2017) 'Buying local can be the saving of our cities', *The Times*, 1 November (www.thetimes.co.uk/article/buying-local-can-be-the-saving-of-our-cities-7j2t9t5zc).

[32] Since the 2017 General Election, Theresa May announced progress towards introducing an energy price cap, although at the time of writing it is not clear whether or not it will be implemented as government policy.

[33] Taylor et al, op cit.

[34] Joseph Rowntree Foundation, op cit.

[35] Cited in Clarke, S. (ed) (2017) *Work in Brexit Britain: Reshaping the nation's labour market*, London: Resolution Foundation, Chapter 6, p 7 (www.resolutionfoundation.org/app/uploads/2017/07/RF-Brexit-ebook-v2.pdf).

[36] Taylor et al, op cit.

[37] Taylor et al, op cit.

[38] Based on job attributes such as job security, interesting job and good opportunities for advancement. See McKay, S. and Simpson, I. (2016) 'Work', in K. Swales et al, *British Social Attitudes 33*, London: NatCen, p 13.

[39] Unpublished BSA analysis: 63 per cent satisfied compared to 82 per cent.

[40] McKay and Simpson, op cit, p 1.

[41] McKay and Simpson, op cit, p 23.

[42] McKay and Simpson, op cit, p 13.

[43] McKay and Simpson, op cit, p 17.

[44] McKay and Simpson, op cit, p 15.

[45] Curtice, op cit, p 2.

[46] Curtice, op cit, p 5.

[47] Kellner, op cit.

[48] Curtice, op cit, p 2.

[49] Curtice, op cit, p 5.

[50] The independent review of modern working practices by Matthew Taylor was commissioned by the government and its recommendations published in July 2017; see Taylor, M. (2017) *Good work: The Taylor review of modern working practices*, London: Department for Business, Energy and Industrial Strategy, 2017, p 89 (www.gov.uk/government/publications/good-work-the-taylor-review-of-modern-working-practices).

[51] Henehan, K. (2017) 'Today's exam question: How do we remedy the growing skills divide?' London: Resolution Foundation, blog, 22 August (www.resolutionfoundation.org/media/blog/todays-exam-question-how-do-we-remedy-the-growing-skills-divide/).

[52] The Joseph Rowntree Foundation has costed a policy to meet all basic skills needs including digital skills by 2030, which would require doubling the current rates of participation from around 100,000 people per year for literacy and numeracy to 200,000 and cost £200 million. See Joseph Rowntree Foundation, op cit.

[53] Policy Exchange recommends a new high-level quality target be established along with an employer-run Institute for Apprenticeships.

[54] The Social Mobility Commission suggests a Second Chance Career Fund to help older workers retrain and write off advanced learner loans for part-time workers taking Level 3 qualifications, and that low-quality apprenticeships are banned altogether; see Social Mobility Commission, op cit, p 125.

[55] Quoted in Mulholland, H. (2012) 'George Osborne: Austerity may last until 2018', *The Guardian*, 8 October (www.theguardian.com/politics/2012/oct/08/george-osborne-austerity-2018).

[56] Quoted in Gentleman, A. (2015) 'Labour vows to reduce reliance on foodbanks if it comes to power', *The Guardian*, 17 March (www.theguardian.com/society/2015/mar/17/labour-vows-to-reduce-reliance-on-food-banks-if-it-comes-to-power).

[57] Hills, J. (2015) *Good times, bad times*, Bristol: Policy Press, p 251.

[58] In 1989, 61% agreed that 'The government should spend more money on welfare benefits for the poor, even if it leads to higher taxes' which fell to 30% in 2014; Taylor, E. and Taylor Gooby, P. (2015) 'Benefits and welfare', in J. Curtice and R. Ormston et al *British Social Attitudes 32*, London: NatCen, p 1.

[59] Clery, E., Lee, L. and Kunz, S. (2013) *Public attitudes to poverty and welfare, 1983-2011: Analysis using British Social Attitudes data*, York: Joseph Rowntree Foundation (www.natcen.ac.uk/media/137637/poverty-and-welfare.pdf).

[60] While the data is prior to the introduction of recent welfare reform, it is not clear that confidence in the welfare system will have improved during the long implementation phase, which has been the subject of frequent criticism. See also DWP (Department for Work and Pensions) (2013) *The Benefit Cap: Public perceptions and pre-implementation effects*, London: DWP, October (www.gov.uk/government/uploads/system/uploads/attachment_data/file/249005/rrep850.pdf).

[61] Clery, E. (2016) 'Welfare', in K. Swales et al, *British Social Attitudes 33*, London: NatCen, p 1.

[62] Taylor et al, op cit, p 21.

[63] Clery, op cit, p 12.

[64] Unpublished analysis of BSA by NatCen for Joseph Rowntree Foundation (2017).

[65] Taylor et al, op cit, p 15.

[66] Clery, op cit, p 5.

[67] Unpublished analysis of BSA by NatCen for Joseph Rowntree Foundation (2017).

[68] Clery, op cit, pp 1, 10.

[69] Clery, op cit, p 7.

[70] Baumberg Geiger et al, op cit, p 10.

[71] Ibid, p 1.

[72] Taylor et al, op cit and unpublished analysis of BSA by NatCen for Joseph Rowntree Foundation (2017).

[73] Kellner, op cit.

74 Unpublished analysis of BSA by NatCen for Joseph Rowntree Foundation (2017).

75 Unpublished analysis of BSA by NatCen for Joseph Rowntree Foundation (2017).

76 Welfare spending in 2016-17 was £213 billion, the same level as it was in 2010-11; OBR (Office for Budget Responsibility (2017) 'An OBR guide to welfare spending' (http://budgetresponsibility.org.uk/forecasts-in-depth/brief-guides-and-explainers/an-obr-guide-to-welfare-spending/).

77 Joseph Rowntree Foundation, op cit.

78 Gandy, K., Streeter Hurle, P., Bustin, C. and Glazebrook, K. (2016) *Poverty and decision-making: How behavioural science can improve opportunity in the UK*, The Behavioural Insights Team (www.behaviouralinsights.co.uk/uncategorized/poverty-and-decision-making-how-behavioural-science-can-improve-opportunity-in-the-uk/).

79 Likki, T. (2017) 'Behavioural insights and the welfare state', The Behavioural Insights Team, quoted in Chwalisz, C., Thillaye, R. and Kinloch, E. (2017) *New routes to social justice*, Policy Network.

80 Fitzpatrick, S., Bramley, G., Sosenko, F., Blenkinsopp, J., Johnsen, S., Littlewood, M., et al (2016) *Destitution in the UK*, I-SPHERE at Herriot Watt University, York: Joseph Rowntree Foundation (www.jrf.org.uk/report/destitution-uk).

81 O'Leary, D. (2013) *Something for something: Restoring a contributory principle to the welfare state*, London: Demos (www.demos.co.uk/files/Something_For_Something_-_DuncanOLeary.pdf).

Chapter 6

1 See Palenciek, J. (2015) 'Public attitudes to inheritance tax', YouGov, 7 January (https://yougov.co.uk/news/2015/01/07/public-attitudes-inheritance-tax/; Frayne, J. (2015) *Overlooked but decisive: Connecting with England's just about managing classes*, London: Policy Exchange (https://policyexchange.org.uk/publication/overlooked-but-decisive-connecting-with-englands-just-about-managing-classes/); Mattinson, D. (2010) *Talking to a brick wall: How New Labour stopped listening to the voter and why we need a new politics*, London: Biteback Publishing.

2 Taylor, E., Saunders, C. and Toomse-Smith, M. (2017) *Social and political attitudes of people on low incomes: 2017 report*, London/York: NatCen for Joseph Rowntree Foundation, p 11.

3 Harding, R. (2017) 'Key findings', in E. Clery, J. Curtice and R. Harding (eds) *British Social Attitudes 34*, London: NatCen, p 10; Swales, K. and Attar Taylor, E. (2017) 'Moral issues', in E. Clery, J. Curtice and R. Harding (eds) *British Social Attitudes 34*, London: NatCen p 1 (www.bsa.natcen.ac.uk/media/39196/bsa34_full-report_fin.pdf).

4 Sixty-eight per cent of working-class people agree with the statement, 'Britain has changed for the worse over the past 20-30 years' compared to 52% of middle-class people. Fifty-seven per cent of middle class people and 62% of working-class people disagree with the statement, 'Worries about

the future are overdone: most children growing up in Britain today will end up better off than their parents'; see Kellner, P. (2014) 'The changing politics of social class', YouGov for *Prospect*, June (https://yougov.co.uk/news/2014/06/09/changing-politics-social-class/).

[5] Johnson, P. (2015) 'Why is the UK's housing benefit bill so high?', BBC News (www.bbc.co.uk/news/business-34290727). Of the 250,000 homes needed, a report for the Joseph Rowntree Foundation estimates that 80,000 of these need to be affordable homes to rent or own; Lupton, M. and Collins, H. (2015) *Living rents – A new development framework for affordable housing*, June, Savills (www.savills.co.uk/blog/article/189220/residential-property/a-living-rent-could-solve-the-housing-crisis.aspx).

[6] Jefferys, P. and Lloyd, T. (2017) *Civic house building*, London: Shelter.

[7] About two-thirds of the decline in the probability of a UK-born household living in social housing is due to undersupply, as opposed to one-third immigration and changed rules; Battinson et al (2014), cited in Vargas-Silva, C., Markaki, Y. and Sumption, M. (2016) *The impacts of international migration on poverty in the UK*, York: Joseph Rowntree Foundation (www.jrf.org.uk/report/impacts-international-migration-poverty-uk).

[8] About 1.25 million people were found to be destitute at some point in 2015, 312,000 of whom were children. Some migrant groups face a disproportionate risk of destitution; however, 79% of those destitute were British-born. See Fitzpatrick, S., Bramley, G., Sosenko, F., Blenkinsopp, J., Johnsen, S., Littlewood, M., et al (2016) *Destitution in the UK*, I-SPHERE at Herriot Watt University, York: Joseph Rowntree Foundation (www.jrf.org.uk/report/destitution-uk).

[9] DCLG (Department for Communities and Local Government) *Fixing our broken housing market*, Housing White Paper (www.gov.uk/government/uploads/system/uploads/attachment_data/file/590464/Fixing_our_broken_housing_market_-_print_ready_version.pdf).

[10] Ipsos MORI, *Issues Monitor*, July 2017.

[11] Abraham, T. (2017) 'The local vs the national: The NHS comes into conflict with Brexit in terms of voters' priorities', YouGov, 7 June (https://yougov.co.uk/news/2017/06/07/local-vs-national-nhs-comes-conflict-brexit-terms-/).

[12] Taylor et al, op cit.

[13] Curtice, J. (2017) 'The role of government', in R. Harding et al, *British Social Attitudes 34*, London: NatCen, p 5.

[14] Taylor et al, op cit.

[15] Husain, F., Jessop, C., Kelley, N., et al (2016) *Social and political attitudes of people on low incomes: 2016 report*, London/York: NatCen for Joseph Rowntree Foundation (http://natcen.ac.uk/media/1345858/social-and-political-attitudes-of-people-on-low-incomes.pdf).

[16] Marshall, B. (2017) 'Public: Housing in crisis but Government can do something', Ipsos MORI for Chartered Institute of Housing, June (www.ipsos.com/ipsos-mori/en-uk/public-housing-crisis-government-can-do-something).

17 National Housing Federation (2017) *Demise of the NIMBY: Changing attitudes to building new homes* (www.housing.org.uk/resource-library/browse/demise-of-the-nimby-changing-attitudes-to-building-new-homes/).

18 DCLG (Department for Communities and Local Government) and Lewis, B. (2014) 'Public opinion shifts behind our housebuilding plans', Press release (www.gov.uk/government/news/public-opinion-shifts-behind-our-house-building-plans).

19 The Conservative 2017 general election manifesto pledged to deliver 1 million new homes between 2015-20 and a further half a million homes by 2022, a rough annual average of 187,500.

20 Jefferys and Lloyd, op cit.

21 ONS Digital (2016) *How is the welfare budget spent?*, Office for National Statistics (http://visual.ons.gov.uk/welfare-spending/).

22 The cost of Housing Benefit in 2009-10 was £20 billion; see OBR (Office for Budget Responsibility) (2017) 'Welfare spending: Housing benefit' (http://budgetresponsibility.org.uk/forecasts-in-depth/tax-by-tax-spend-by-spend/welfare-spending-housing-benefit/).

23 Bessis, H. (2016) 'Mapping stamp duty and the housing benefit bill', Centre for Cities (www.centreforcities.org/blog/mapping-stamp-duty-and-the-housing-benefit-bill/).

24 Ford, R. and Lymperopoulou, R. (2017) 'Immigration', in R. Harding et al, *British Social Attitudes 34*, London: NatCen, p 3 (www.bsa.natcen.ac.uk/media/39196/bsa34_full-report_fin.pdf).

25 Rutter, J. (2015) *Moving up and getting on: Migration, integration and social cohesion in the UK*, Bristol: Policy Press, p 18.

26 Casey, L. (2016) *The Casey Review: A review into opportunity and integration*, p 8 (www.gov.uk/government/uploads/system/uploads/attachment_data/file/575973/The_Casey_Review_Report.pdf).

27 Rutter, op cit, p 18.

28 Pidd, H. (2012) 'Census reveals rural town of Boston has most eastern European immigrants', *The Guardian*, 11 December (www.theguardian.com/uk/2012/dec/11/census-boston-eastern-european-immigration).

29 Analysis by *The Economist* (2016) 'Britain's immigration paradox' (www.economist.com/news/britain/21701950-areas-lots-migrants-voted-mainly-remain-or-did-they-britains-immigration-paradox).

30 Casey, op cit, p 7.

31 Ipsos MORI (2017) 'The NHS and EU/Brexit have risen in concern', *Issues Monitor,* July (www.slideshare.net/IpsosMORI/ipsos-mori-issues-index-july-2017-78228550).

32 Taylor et al, op cit.

33 Ford and Lymperopoulou, op cit, pp 1-2.

34 Ibid, and the rest of data in this section.

35 Husain et al, op cit.

36 A qualitative in-depth study of people on low incomes in an outer London borough, conducted by NatCen and published in Husain et al, op cit.

37 Rutter, op cit, p 214.

[38] See, for example, TUC (Trades Union Congress) (2007) 'Migrant agency workers in the UK' (www.tuc.org.uk/research-analysis/reports/migrant-agency-workers-uk).

[39] Polls show a variable picture of the extent to which people support stopping immigration altogether, so the results may be dependent on how the question is asked.

[40] Lord Ashcroft (2013) 'Public opinion and the politics of immigration', Lord Ashcroft Polls, 1 September (http://lordashcroftpolls.com/2013/09/public-opinion-and-the-politics-of-immigration/).

[41] Runnymede Trust submission to the Casey Review, Omar Khan and Nissa Finney, University of St Andrews, 2016 (www.runnymedetrust.org/uploads/CaseyReviewLetter.pdf).

[42] ONS Digital (2015) 'People who cannot speak English well are more likely to be in poor health', Office for National Statistics (https://visual.ons.gov.uk/language-census-2011).

[43] APPG (All-Party Parliamentary Group) on Social Integration (2017) *Final report into integration of immigrants: Integration not demonisation* (www.socialintegrationappg.org.uk/reports).

[44] Casey, op cit, p 48.

[45] Blair, T. (1995) Leader's speech, Labour Party Conference, Brighton, 1995 (www.britishpoliticalspeech.org/speech-archive.htm?speech=201).

[46] Crime Survey of England and Wales and Home Office data quoted in Lammy, D. (2015) *Low crime for all: How to reduce crime for London's communities*, London: Policy Exchange and Capital City Foundation (www.policyexchange.org.uk/wp-content/uploads/2016/09/low-crime-for-all-how-to-reduce-crime-fo-londons-communities.pdf).

[47] Ipsos MORI, *Issues Monitor*, July 2017.

[48] Husain et al, op cit.

[49] Husain et al, op cit.

[50] Taylor et al, op cit.

[51] Husain et al, op cit.

[52] Clery, E. and Mead, J. (2017) 'Civil liberties', in R. Harding et al, *British Social Attitudes 34*, London: NatCen, pp 2, 24.

[53] Frayne, op cit.

[54] Forty-three per cent of those in the lowest income category support the death penalty, followed by 53% of the second quintile, 48% of the third income quintile, 41% of the fourth and 39% of those in the highest income quintile; see Taylor et al, op cit.

[55] Kellner, op cit.

[56] Clery and Mead, op cit, p 13.

[57] Clery and Mead, op cit, p 20.

[58] Ford and Lymperopoulou, op cit, p 7.

[59] Frayne, op cit.

[60] Gash, T. (2016) *Criminal: The truth about why people do bad things*, London: Allen Lane.

61 What Works (2012) 'What is the best thing the police can do to reduce crime?', part of the 'What Works in policing to reduce crime' series, What Works Centre, National College of Policing, 2012 (http://whatworks. college.police.uk/Research/overview/Pages/best.aspx).

62 In an evidence review by the What Works Centre National College of Policing of the 'Zero Tolerance' policing approach, organisational goals, plans and accountability were found to be the components of success in crime reduction in New York during the 1990s, as well as a focus on quality of life issues, problem-solving and targeting of crime hot spots; What Works (2012) 'Evidence on zero-tolerance policing', part of the 'What Works in policing to reduce crime' series, What Works Centre National College of Policing (http://whatworks.college.police.uk/Research/overview/ Documents/WW_overview_Zero_tolerance.pdf).

63 BBC News (2017) 'Reality check: Are there 20,000 fewer police?' (http:// www.bbc.co.uk/news/uk-politics-39779288)

64 Casciani, D. (2016) 'Police and Crime Commissioners: Unloved but re-elected', BBC News, 9 May (www.bbc.co.uk/news/uk-politics-36248972).

65 What Works, op cit.

66 What Works (2012) 'Targeted approaches to crime and disorder reduction', part of the 'What Works in policing to reduce crime' series, What Works Centre National College of Policing.

67 Conservative candidate for London, Mayor Zac Goldsmith, accused his opponent of links to extremists, and wrote an article for the *Daily Mail* headlined 'On Thursday, are we really going to hand the world's greatest city to a Labour Party that thinks terrorists is its friends?' and this was illustrated with the bus that was blown up in the 2005 London terror attack. Goldsmith issued leaflets targeted at specific ethnic groups, for example, one aimed at the 'British Indian community', and said of Labour candidate Sadiq Khan, 'His party supports a wealth tax on family jewellery'; see Gani, A. (2016) 'Zac Goldsmith criticised over leaflet aimed at British Indians', *The Guardian*, 16 March (www.theguardian.com/politics/2016/mar/16/ zac-goldsmith-leaflet-british-indians-heirlooms).

Chapter 7

1 Robert Dahl, quoted in Dalton, R.J. (2017) *The participation gap: Social status and political inequality*, Oxford: Oxford University Press, p 4.

2 Described by Robert Putnam as 'bowling alone'; see Putnam, R. (2000) *Bowling alone: The collapse and revival of American community*, New York: Simon & Schuster.

3 Mount, F. (2012) *Mind the gap: The new class divide in Britain*, London: Short Books, p 273.

4 Ibid, p 273.

5 'In the 1970s, four out of five people believed that unions wielded too much power, but today only one in three voters do.'' Cited in Kelly, G. (2017) 'Rebooting the rank and file: Why there's still hope for the unions',

Prospect Magazine, 9 October (www.prospectmagazine.co.uk/magazine/rebooting-the-rank-and-file-gavin-kelly-trade-unions).

[6] Scott Paul, A. (2015) 'Playing the media's "poke fun at people in poverty" game gets us nowhere', Joseph Rowntree Foundation blog, 16 January (www.jrf.org.uk/blog/playing-media's-'poke-fun-people-poverty'-game-gets-us-nowhere).

[7] Tyler, I. (2008) 'Chav mum, chav scum: Class disgust in contemporary Britain', *Feminist Media Studies*, vol 8, no 1, pp 17-34.

[8] Jones, O. (2011) *Chavs: The demonization of the working class*, London: Verso, pp 2, 233.

[9] Goodwin, M. and Heath, O. (2016) *Brexit vote explained: Poverty, low skills and lack of opportunities*, York: Joseph Rowntree Foundation (www.jrf.org.uk/report/brexit-vote-explained-poverty-low-skills-and-lack-opportunities).

[10] Curtice, J. (2017) 'The vote to leave the EU', in R. Harding et al *British Social Attitudes 34*, London: NatCen, p 5 (www.bsa.natcen.ac.uk/media/39196/bsa34_full-report_fin.pdf).

[11] Quote from Goodwin, M.J. and Ford, R.. (2014) 'White face, blue collar, grey hair: The "left behind" voters only UKIP understands', *The Guardian*, 5 March (www.theguardian.com/commentisfree/2014/mar/05/left-behind-voters-only-ukip-understands); Goodwin, M. and Ford, R. (2014) *Revolt on the right*, London: Routledge

[12] Husain, F., Jessop, C., Kelley, N., et al (2016) *Social and political attitudes of people on low incomes: 2016 report*, London/York: NatCen for Joseph Rowntree Foundation, pp 8-9 (http://natcen.ac.uk/media/1345858/social-and-political-attitudes-of-people-on-low-incomes.pdf).

[13] Curtice, J. (2016) 'Politics', in K. Swales et al, *British Social Attitudes 33*, London: NatCen, pp 11, 12.

[14] Taylor, E., Saunders, C. and Toomse-Smith, M. (2017) *Social and political attitudes of people on low incomes: 2017 report*, London/York: NatCen for Joseph Rowntree Foundation, p 25.

[15] For example, 58% of those on low incomes compared to 77% of the general public were likely to vote in the 2015 general election; see Husain et al, op cit, p 35.

[16] Taylor et al, op cit, p 26.

[17] Dalton, op cit.

[18] Unpublished analysis for Joseph Rowntree Foundation by NatCen (2017).

[19] Ibid.

[20] Kellner, P. (2014) 'The changing politics of social class', YouGov for *Prospect*, June (https://yougov.co.uk/news/2014/06/09/changing-politics-social-class/).

[21] Husain et al, op cit, p 7.

[22] Ibid.

[23] More detailed analysis from a qualitative depth study by NatCen for Joseph Rowntree Foundation that formed part of Husain et al, op cit.

[24] Husain et al, op cit, pp 10, 42.

[25] Taylor et al, op cit, p 28.

[26] Ibid.

[27] Goodwin, M. and Heath, O. (2017) *UK General Election vote examined: Income, poverty and Brexit*, York: Joseph Rowntree Foundation (www.jrf. org.uk/report/uk-2017-general-election-vote-examined).

[28] Taylor et al, op cit, p 28.

[29] Sixty-one per cent of those on the lowest incomes agree with the statement that ordinary working people do not get their fair share; 62% on the second income quintile agree; 62% on the third income quintile; 55% of the fourth highest income quintile; and 51% of the highest income group. Unpublished analysis for Joseph Rowntree Foundation by NatCen (2017).

[30] While there are no income differences in how authoritarian people are, NatCen found that there were differences on views on the death penalty. The second and third income groups are most likely to say that the death penalty is appropriate for some cases, with the poorest and richest fifth less likely to agree. See Taylor et al, op cit, p 29.

[31] Evans, G. and Mellon, J. (2016) 'Social class: Identity, awareness and political attitudes: Why are we still working class?', in J. Curtice, M. Phillips and E. Clery (eds) *British Social Attitudes 33*, London: NatCen.

[32] Curtice, op cit, 'Politics', p 1.

[33] Ibid, p 1, 11. Around 20% of voters in England think England should have its own parliament; another 20% think each region should have its own assembly that runs services such as health.

[34] Husain et al, op cit, p 12.

[35] Curtice, op cit, p 7. Around 40% of voters in Scotland support independence (not in the UK) and less than 10% support the UK with no devolution. These figures will be more variable over time as support for independence has increased since 2010.

[36] Scottish Government (2016) *Scottish Social Attitudes 2015: Attitudes to government, the National Health Service, the economy and standard of living*, Edinburgh: ScotCen, p 9.

[37] Ibid, p 11.

[38] Scully, R. (2017) 'What has devolution ever done for us?', Cardiff: Wales Governance Centre, Cardiff University (http://sites.cardiff.ac.uk/wgc/2017/09/19/what-has-devolution-ever-done-for-us/).

[39] Scottish Government, op cit, p 12.

[40] Scottish Government, op cit, p 17.

[41] Stoker, G. and Hay, C. (2017) 'Understanding and challenging populist negativity towards politics: The perspectives of British citizens', *Political Studies*, vol 65, issue 1, March.

[42] Survey results in Stoker and Hay, ibid. The full research findings are in the Hansard Society's *Audit of political engagement 9*, parts I and II, London: Hansard Society.

[43] Data is from the survey for Stoker and Hay, ibid, showing, for example, 28% favoured 'change processes of politics to make it more accountable and to ensure that what is promised is delivered', 16% favoured 'give citizens more of a say', 9% said 'institutional changes to parliament, constitution reform or

changes to electoral system' and 4% said 'get politicians to be more normal.'
In a second question, where voters were asked to pick up to three options,
48% said 'make politics more transparent so that it is easier to follow', 39%
said 'make politicians more accountable for their performance between
elections', 8% said constitutional changes and 6% said 'more people like
me as MPs.' See the original source for the full set of answers.

44   Flinders, M. (2012) *Defending politics: Why democracy matters in the twenty-first
      century*, Oxford: Oxford University Press, p 14.
45   Vivyan, N. and Wagner, M. (2015) 'What do voters want from their local
      MP?', *Political Quarterly*, vol 86, no 1, January-March. The research was
      conducted on the role of an MP, although there is no reason to suggest
      lessons could not also be drawn for constituency members of the Scottish
      Parliament or Welsh Assembly.
46   BritainThinks (2017) 'What does Britain want from its leaders?' (http://
      britainthinks.com/news/what-does-britain-want-in-a-leader).
47   Mattinson, D. (2010) *Talking to a brick wall: How New Labour stopped listening
      to the voter and why we need a new politics*, London: Biteback Publishing, pp
      310, 312.
48   Ibid, p 199.
49   See Hansard Society (2017) *Audit of political engagement* London: Hansard
      Society (www.hansardsociety.org.uk/research/audit-of-political-
      engagement), which reports that there has been no 'EU referendum effect'
      similar to that of the independence referendum in Scotland, and knowledge
      of and interest in politics have declined since the previous year.
50   Russell J. Dalton argues in *The participation gap*, p 4, that the social
      participation gap is actually larger for non-electoral forms of political
      participation such as deliberative democracy. For recommendations on
      improving institutional inclusivity in deliberative approaches, see Patel, R.
      (2017) *Citizens, participation and economics – Emerging findings from the Citizens'
      Economic Council*, RSA (www.thersa.org/discover/publications-and-articles/
      rsa-blogs/2017/11/citizens-participation-and-economics--emerging-
      findings-from-the-citizens-economic-council). See also www.thersa.org/
      globalassets/pdfs/reports/rsa-citizen-participation-and-the-economy.pdf
51   Kelly, op cit.
52   See Stoker, G. (2006) *Why politics matters: Making democracy work*, Basingstoke:
      Palgrave Macmillan, pp 104-11.
53   Norris, E. and Adam, R. (2017) *All change: Why Britain is so prone to policy
      reinvention, and what can be done about it*, London: Institute for Government,
      p 23 (www.instituteforgovernment.org.uk/sites/default/les/publications/
      IfG_All_change_report_FINAL.pdf).
54   As advocated by the Institute for Government: see Norris, E. and Adam,
      R. (2017) *All change: Why Britain is so prone to policy reinvention, and
      what can be done about it*, London: Institute for Government, p 4 (www.
      instituteforgovernment.org.uk/sites/default/files/publications/IfG_All_
      change_report_FINAL.pdf).

55 Defined as either in favour of leaving the EU or repatriating some powers; Curtice, op cit, 'The vote to leave the EU' (see www.bsa.natcen.ac.uk/media/39149/bsa34_brexit_final.pdf).

56 Goodwin, M. and Milazzo, C. (2015) 'Britain, the European Union and the Referendum: What drives Euroscepticism?', Briefing, London: Chatham House, December (www.chathamhouse.org/sites/files/chathamhouse/publications/research/20151209EuroscepticismGoodwinMilazzo.pdf).

57 Husain et al, op cit, Figure 8.

58 Curtice, op cit, p 8 (see www.bsa.natcen.ac.uk/media/39149/bsa34_brexit_final.pdf).

Chapter 8

1 Gordon Brown speech to Labour Party Conference, 24 September 2007 (full text: http://news.bbc.co.uk/1/hi/uk_politics/7010664.stm)

2 Theresa May speech to Conservative Party Conference 5 October 2016 (full text: www.independent.co.uk/news/uk/politics/theresa-may-speech-tory-conference-2016-in-full-transcript-a7346171.html)

Figure sources

1   Identifying with a political party
      Taylor, E., Saunders, C. and Toomse-Smith, M. (2017) *Social and political attitudes of people on low incomes, 2017 report*, London: NatCen Social Research, Figure 6.3 (www.bsa.natcen.ac.uk/media/39207/social-and-political-attitudes-of-people-on-low-incomes-2017-full-report.pdf).

2   How the working class voted, 1964-2015
      Goodwin, M. and Heath, O. (2017) *UK 2017 General Election vote examined: Income, poverty and Brexit*, York: Joseph Rowntree Foundation (www.jrf.org.uk/report/uk-2017-general-election-vote-examined).

3   Profile of income groups by age, gender and education
      Taylor et al, op cit, Figure 2.1.

4   New working class groupings
      Savage, M. (2015) *Social class in the 21st century*, London: Pelican, Tables 5.1, 5.2 and Figure 7.2.

5   Rating values, by social class
      Frayne, J. (2015) *Overlooked but decisive: Connecting with England's just about managing classes*, London: Policy Exchange (https://policyexchange.org.uk/publication/overlooked-but-decisive-connecting-with-englands-just-about-managing-classes/).

6   Public values compared to those associated with Conservatives and Labour
      Frayne, ibid.

7   Six most frequent worries or concerns, according to income
      Taylor et al, op cit, Figure 3.2.

8   What do the public want from the education system?
      Tanner, E. and Kelley, N. (2017) *Attitudes towards 'good schools' and selective education*, London: NatCen Social Research (http://natcen.ac.uk/our-research/research/attitudes-towards-%E2%80%98good-schools%E2%80%99-selective-education/).

Dahlgreen, W. (2016) 'Fewer than 1 in 5 teachers think academies improve education', YouGov (https://yougov.co.uk/news/2016/03/17/teachers-critical-academies/).

9   Public support for funding the NHS
Wellings, D. (2017) 'The politics of health: What do the public think about the NHS', London: The King's Fund (www.kingsfund.org.uk/publications/articles/politics-health).

10   Wage map of Britain
ONS (Office for National Statistics) (2015) 'What are the average earnings where you work?', Annual Survey of Hours and Earnings (www.ons.gov.uk/visualisations/nesscontent/dvc126/).

11   Support for redistribution, according to income
Taylor et al, op cit, Figure 4.2.

12   Public attitudes to the government's role in the economy
Curtice, J. (2017) 'Role of government', in Clery, E., Curtice, J. and Harding, R. (eds) British Social Attitudes 34, London: NatCen, pp 67-84 (www.bsa.natcen.ac.uk/media/39145/bsa34_role-of-govt_final.pdf).

13   Working status, according to income
Taylor et al, op cit, Figure 2.3.

14   Jobs in modern Britain
ONS (Office for National Statistics) (2017) 'Dataset: EMP04: Employment by occupation' (www.ons.gov.uk/employmentandlabourmarket/peopleinwork/employmentandemployeetypes/datasets/employmentbyoccupationemp04).

15   What people experienced in work, 2005-15
McKay, S. and Simpson, I. (2016) 'Work', in J. Curtice, M. Phillips and E. Clery (eds) British Social Attitudes 33, London, NatCen (www.bsa.natcen.ac.uk/media/39061/bsa33_work.pdf).

16   Social security spending in 2016
ONS (Office for National Statistics) Digital (2016) 'How is the welfare budget spent?' (https://visual.ons.gov.uk/welfare-spending/).

17   Percentage believing people who get social security 'don't really deserve any help', according to income
Taylor et al, op cit, Figure 5.2.

Figure sources

18   Number of homes built, 1980-2015
ONS (Office for National Statistics) Digital (2016) 'UK Perspectives 2016: Housing and home ownership in the UK' (https://visual.ons.gov.uk/uk-perspectives-2016-housing-and-home-ownership-in-the-uk/).

19   Migration to and from the UK and net migration, 1975-2016
Rutter, J. (2015) *Moving up and getting on: Migration integration and social cohesion in the UK*, Bristol: Policy Press, Figure 2.1, originally sourced from Office for National Statistics' long-term international migration statistics.

Source for 2014-16: www.ons.gov.uk/peoplepopulationandcommunity/populationandmigration/internationalmigration

20   Those saying immigration is among their current concerns, according to income
Taylor et al, op cit, Figure 3.2.

21   Interest in politics, according to income
Taylor et al (2017), op cit, Figure 6.1.

22   Public attitudes-led policy-making
Original figure by Claire Ainsley (2017).

Index

Note: Page numbers in italic indicate a figure.

Manufactured by Amazon.ca
Bolton, ON

13300051R00116